Walk Upon a Time:
An Appalachian Trail Thru-Hike
By Leslie Fletcher

WALK UPON A TIME: AN APPALACHIAN TRAIL THRU-HIKE

First edition. February 23, 2023.

ISBN: 979-8215082041

Written by Leslie Fletcher.

Glossary

Appalachian Trail (AT): A 2,200-mile long-distance hiking trail that runs from Georgia to Maine.

Blaze: A marking on a tree or rock that indicates the trail.

Thru-hiker: Someone who hikes the entire length of a long-distance trail from end to end.

Trail Angel: A person who provides assistance to hikers, such as a ride into town or a place to stay.

Nero: A day of hiking with very few miles, allowing for more rest.

Zero: A day of no hiking, usually spent in town resupplying or resting.

Shelter: A designated camping area with a shelter for hikers to sleep under.

Thru-hiker hobble: A limp caused by sore feet or blisters.

White blaze: The trail marking used on the Appalachian Trail.

Hiker hunger: A ravenous appetite caused by long-distance hiking.

Trail name: A nickname given to a hiker by other hikers on the trail.

Trail register: A book at a trailhead or shelter for hikers to sign and leave notes.

Leave No Trace: A set of principles that promote outdoor ethics and responsible hiking.

Hiker midnight: A term used to describe the time when hikers typically go to bed on the trail, usually around 9 pm.

Reroute: A change to the trail's official route due to natural events or construction.

Section hiker: Someone who hikes the trail in smaller sections over time instead of all at once.

Hostel - a type of accommodation that caters specifically to hikers, providing basic amenities like showers, laundry facilities, and sometimes even meals.

Blue blaze - a side trail that connects to the Appalachian Trail, often used as a shortcut or to access a particular viewpoint or shelter.

Trail magic - an unexpected act of kindness from someone (often a stranger) that makes a hiker's day, like a cooler of cold drinks left on the side of the trail or a hot meal offered at a road crossing.

SOBO - short for "southbound," refers to hikers who are hiking the trail from Maine to Georgia (opposite direction of NOBO).

NOBO - short for "northbound," refers to hikers who are hiking the trail from Georgia to Maine (most common direction).

Flip-flop - a thru-hiking strategy that involves starting at one point on the trail, hiking to a midpoint, then jumping to the opposite end of the trail and hiking back to the midpoint.

Slackpacking: Hiking with a light daypack or no pack at all, while your main pack is transported to your next destination.

Yogi-ing: A technique used to get food or other supplies from other hikers or day-hikers without directly asking for it, by making friendly conversation and subtly mentioning your needs.

Green Tunnel: A section of the trail that is densely wooded and lacks scenic vistas.

Triple Crown: The achievement of completing the three longest trails in the United States - the Appalachian Trail, the Pacific Crest Trail, and the Continental Divide Trail.

Rain-fly: Covering for tent in inclement weather

Introduction

The following is the day-to-day account of my 2016 Appalachian Trail thru-hike.

April 10, 2016

In the car with mom for the last little bit of a drive to Georgia. Meeting up with my brother John Bradley in Chattanooga. Super thrilled they could join me for the start. What an honor. Picking up some last-minute gear (map!) and off to the trailhead! Looks a little damp out there, so I will try to stay dry and check in from the tent tonight. Happy Trails!

April 11, 2016

First day, first snag! Somewhere along the line I decided the right choice would be to embark on a multi season hike without the rainfly for my tent. I WAS trying to shave some pack weight, but geez. So, shelters for me until Hiawassee, GA, where my rainfly and more food await. Thanks daddy-o! I was stopped today on the trail, taping my toes (I get hotspots!), when a fellow hiker came along. We exchanged the usual "Going to Maine?", "Where did you start today?" and "How are you feeling?" conversation bits, and then David pointed out my water. "You have ALOT of water", he said bluntly. "Well, I drink alot of water...", I trailed off without confidence. "Haven't you noticed here is water....", he began. "EVERYWHERE!", I bemoaned, cutting him off as I realized what people meant when they say you pack your fears. My fear happens to weigh alot. "Yeah", he laughed, "It's coming out of the sides of the mountains!". So I dumped a liter and a half, drank a half liter and reserved a quarter liter for the duration of my hike. And I flew! Arrived at the shelter in just enough time to squeeze in (thanks guys!). It's bustling and cheerful here. And even though I'm not contributing to the conversation, it's helping me just being here with others who are struggling how I am struggling and conquering what I'm conquering. So warm and cozy. No rainfly? No problem!

April 12, 2016

Lots of laughter this morning in Shelter Gooch! Good people, good stories, good vibes! So, I realized this morning, that because of the rainfly situation, I would have to stay in a hostel tonight (gasp). The next closest shelters require a bear canister, which I opted not to bring. So instead of attempting 24 miles in one day, I will suck it up and stay in a hostel. Beautiful, short hike today. I didn't even make it to the road proper before I had hitched a ride from the trail into town. Thanks, stranger!! So far this has been a fantastic experience! Sharing laundry loads, dinner and lives. The range of types of people hiking with me is large. Men, women, North Americans, Europeans, Asians, South Americans, Australians. It's neat. All kinds of experiences and motivations brought us here. And we are ALL stoked to be here and talk about gear and the trail with others who are consumed by these topics, as well. We are nerds, that's for sure! So, a whole pizza, two bananas, two liters of water, a load of laundry and a shower later, I'm feeling like a queen. Thanks to everyone who is as excited about this as I am back home!

April 13, 2016

Today I will slack pack from Woody Gap to Neel's Gap (approx. 11 miles), courtesy of the hiker hostel. I will pick up my pack at Neel's and attempt the 7-mile hike to Whitley Shelter before nightfall. My longest day yet! The slack packing will let me fly! If you aren't familiar, slack packing is a team effort and allows the hiker to drop their heavy pack and hike a certain distance with only water and snacks. Another generous party then shuttles the heavy pack to a point further down trail for pick up. This could spoil me!

April 14, 2016

Made it to Whitley! "Lightning" (a fellow hostel stayer) and I yo-yoed the whole 18.8 miles to Whitley, which was nice. Occasional company seems to be good for moral! We jetted into the shelter and were the first to arrive! I started a fire while Lightning hung his hammock. We spread our gear out and prepared camp as four other familiar faces trickled in. Rambo, Driggatron, James and Ken (no trail names yet). So, once again, super pleasant evening! I was planning on a two-day push to Dicks Creek, where my food and rainfly await, but I might stretch that to three days as I feel possible tightness in my right shin and do NOT need shin splints. We'll see how it goes. So now I'm last out of camp...taking a lazy morning and getting some tech time in while eating oatmeal and drinking coffee by the fire. #thelife! I feel so lucky to be attempting this hike! It's such exquisite torture. Hopefully, I'll get some great pics on this brisk, partly sunny day!! Oh, fun fact about Whitley Shelter! This shelter is listed as 1.2 miles off the trail. Impossible. It's at least 2-2.5 and, at the end of a long day, that's enough to make anyone indignant. Indignant may be too soft a word.

April 15, 2016

Whew. Today's hike was mostly ridgeline, which was dreamy. I felt the Last of the Mohicans theme song playing everywhere I looked and longed for moccasins and deerskin leggings. When did I ever not, really?

So, I have a crew. It's a small crew, and temporary, but it's a crew. We hike at different paces and rarely together, but during these early days, we group plan around fires, talk everyone's resupply, shower/laundry, and schedule needs. Inevitably, we all decide "we will see how I feel in the morning". Lol. It really IS day by day.

There is a triple crowner (she has thru-hiked the Pacific Crest Trail and the Continental Divide Trail and is now attempting the Appalachian Trail. The "triple crown" of North American thru hiking!) at the shelter tonight! So cool! Hearing her talk only increases the gnawing hunger that I must try it myself. It's nice to have another girl around, one with a plethora of trail miles logged, to observe her routine and maybe pick up some tips. She's a queen and is rocking it!

So, Ken, Driggatron and I have all reserved bunks at Top of Georgia Hostel in Hiawassee, GA for Saturday night. I have opted on the side of caution and will cover the 20 miles from here to the hostel (and RAINFLY!) In two days instead of one. Shins were tight this morning. I've been stretching them, etc., so hopefully I can walk it off. Literally. So, three more nights with community, and I'm tenting it for most of the hike. I can find a rhythm and get back on schedule to make my August 3rd flight! Yippee!

April 15, 2016

So much for 8–10-mile days to start with...and I'm feeling it. Lol, hiking with 19-year-olds is HARD! Did I mention that "Slam" (the triple crowner) is only 19?! Get. It. Girl.

A lovely, rolling hike today. These Georgia mountains are filled with magic. The trees are still barren from winter and there is no undergrowth, but WILDFLOWERS! I find myself stopping constantly to bend down and study these perfect, pristine works of art that proudly decorate their dusty brown surroundings. So small and delicate. And yet they are the first to seek the sun and brave the harsh mountain conditions each spring. Absolutely marvelous!

Ken and I hiked together today. He's rocking some gnarly blisters and I have a tight left calf, so we took it as slow as possible for so many miles. Kate lunched with us on Trey Mountain midst the exposed rock and rhododendron. We had met Kate briefly, earlier that morning while enjoying a trail magic breakfast of sausage, bacon and grilled honey buns(!). Thank you, Art and Jean from Memphis! Their son thru hiked in 2010 and they love coming up in the spring to pay it forward. Their son and two of his friends from the hike six years ago were there as well. It was a heartwarming and inspiring scene!

Kate teaches English in Boston and is here, as she says, "for the epic adventure". Need I say more about this charming gal?! She has set a pretty mild pace for herself, and I'm bummed, cause I would like to encounter her more often on the trail!

Lots of talk of trails around the world tonight. Everyone is excited by this topic. Lol, you would think we were doing something a little more glamorous than mere walking.

My body just disagreed with that last statement. So maybe not mere walking....

April 16, 2016

Easy, breezy 4-mile jaunt to Dicks Creek Gap where Slam, Chaco Rep and I sprawled on the side of the highway like the vagabonds we are to wait for our shuttle. Lots of friendly faces on the trail today! Day hikers, section hikers, thru-hikers and section hikers. All of us delighting in each other and the treasure that is the AT.

The hostel is delightful! So clean and beautiful, welcoming and comforting. Picking up some icy hot, ChapStick and a comb! Luxuries! Lol. My rainfly is finally packed up tight in my pack and I have five more days of food! My next drop is in 100 miles. We'll see how accurate my planning was! So full of a lasagna/spaghetti dinner and guess who arrived at the hostel? KATE! She's having broccoli and asparagus...somebody misses their veggies! So, relaxing in a rocker, watching a game of Frisbee and trying to relax my stiff back and stretch my hamstrings. I'm thinking about something Slam said yesterday when I asked her how she did it. "False confidence", she replied quickly. "Ahh", I murmured noncommittally. How can confidence be false when you accomplish what you set out to accomplish? Should any sort of confidence simply be taken as confidence and run with? Whether it is self-doubt, other's doubts or impossible odds- anything that tries to make you think your confidence is somehow false, needs to be tossed off the side of a cliff like that piece of heavy gear you can no longer tolerate. Embrace your intelligence, your wit, your ingenuity, your courage, your brokenness, your lack of knowledge or ability, your unpreparedness, your fears, your doubts. These are what will allow you to take anything that is thrown your way, accept it, master it and make it a victory in the way that only you can. Nobody else. Only you. So, Slam, here's to you and your rock solid, totally founded confidence. Don't let anyone, including yourself, tell you your confidence is false. Victory is not always as it appears.

April 18, 2016

Think I might need to replace my Anker charger with the solar one if I'm going to have a shot at daily journal entries. Or read the instructions.

Spent the night of the 17th at Standing Indian shelter. Nice night. Lots of military guys. It's inspiring and I feel so honored to be in the company of these hikers. The ones "walking off the war".

It's Slam, Chaco Rep, Crocodile (Ken) and I again tonight. Hung a good-looking bear bag tonight, "PCT" style. Dad, you would be proud. We attempted a two-tree hang, at first. Alas, too much weight made it kind of ineffective. Dinner was spent chatting with a charismatic couple from South Africa. It's so interesting to hear a foreigner's perspective of America, and to hear about their homes! These guys are drawn to the space and openness America has. How undeveloped it is compared to a lot of other countries.

The seventeen-mile hike on the 18th to the Long Branch shelter was nice and tough. Slam and I hiked most of it together. Pushing the pace but taking our time when we halted for one reason or another. We discussed so many topics. Some trivial, some heart-wrenching. It's so freeing being out here. Everything about the trail is just so darn honest.

Slam, Chaco Rep and I jovially breezed three miles down the trail to the shuttle pickup point into Franklin this morning. Talking mostly ground squirrels and giant spiders. We have an award-winning screenplay in the works. Ron (who owns the Budget Inn and hostel in town) regaled about eleven of us with details about town and what to expect further down the trail as we hurtled down to Franklin in his trusty (?) van. Thanks Ron! This is our last town stop for a while, so we're resupplying and picking up mail drops, hitting the local brewery (pint glass headed your way, sis!), doing group laundry, and slamming homemade milkshakes before crashing at the Budget Inn. Up early tomorrow to "embrace the brutality", as they say on the CDT.

April 19, 2016

Feeling good after a "Nero" (an almost zero day). Franklin was great! Everyone was over-the-top friendly and helpful. The postal worker, the convenience store clerk and Ron all went above and beyond to help me, personally. Another super cool trail town experience!

Great hike today. Covered almost fifteen miles of some decent elevation change. So many beautiful streams in this stretch! The lower the trail, the greener you see and it's so thrilling. Watching spring creep in. Slam and I hiked a steady 3 mph today. Took three nice, solid breaks and hiked continuously between. Covered one four mile stretch in an hour!! Which had us giggling because we BOTH had felt super drowsy from lunch break and BOTH of us had unintentionally over compensated. We are supposed to be taking it easy for at least one more week and I am trying so hard to do so!

There is a stone tower on the top of Wayah Bald that has stunning views! There was a wildfire in the valley to the east and a glimpse of Clingmans Dome to the northwest! It was such a pretty view that it had Slam and me bouncing cheerily all the way down to the shelter (which was full. Tent sites and all.) No sweat. Slam and I are kickin' it cowboy style (no tent) about a quarter mile down the trail. Had a nice fire and dinner, hung the bear bag and now I'm watching the fire die, listening to the coyotes nearby and watching for the full moon to peek through cloud cover. Hope it doesn't rain, but just in case, we pitched one tent nearby to throw sleeping bags into quickly. I can't believe it hasn't rained since the first day! It's been gorgeous!

I told Slam "The Horse and His Boy", by C.S. Lewis today while hiking. Took a good hour and we both enjoyed it. Slam read a T.S. Eliot poem after dinner. Did not take an hour and we both also enjoyed it. Win-win.

Trying to camp just before NOC tomorrow and then head into Robbinsville the next day and pick up a food drop! Yay!

April 20, 2016

Opened my eyes at 6am to the sight of a furry, little mouse scurrying right past my sleeping bag. Made me smile. If he doesn't think I'm sharing food, I'm more than happy to play the Cinderella game! No rain last night, so Slam and I stayed warm and dry under the stars. Er, clouds. Oatmeal and coffee for breakfast while we chatted with hikers passing by on the trail. Jack (from London!) and Chaco Rep happened to be a part of our bevy of morning callers. Always fun to see friends! Met so many cool peeps today! Shout out to Tennessee, Mowgli, Exterminator and Kimberly! Y'all are killing it!

There is a father out here hiking the first section of the trail with his son, who will continue to Maine after they part at Nantahala Outdoor Center. This kind of thing really warms my heart. And Storm! Carrying the walking stick of a recently deceased father of a friend all the way to Maine because it was this man's dream for so many years and he never saw it fulfilled. But now this father's treasured walking stick WILL see Katahdin because of one man's kindness. Enough to give me goosebumps. These are the inspiring stories one hears on a DAILY basis out here on the trail and yet another reason I'm losing my heart to this grand adventure.

Hiking with someone as impressive as Slam is turning out to be a blast! Not only is she triple crowning at 19, she is probably the youngest to solo the CDT and her mother is a triple crowner as well! What a rich heritage! I take every chance I can to brag about her!

Today I set the pace. I was worried that I was going too fast, so I asked if I could go first, in order to slow it down. Hah. Turns out I push it even harder! An easy 15-mile day turned into a grueling 19, when I decided to push on past NOC (I KNEW I would want to zero and kayak with Chaco Rep the next day if I stayed!) and find water and flat ground to camp on before the forecasted rain hit. Two and a half miles of vertical trail later, I found a spot not listed in the guide! Perfection. And it was already occupied by Exterminator and his mother. Oh, and his mother! Kimberly mentioned Jennifer Pharr Davis and I nearly flipped. We talked about Jennifer and how she is so inspiring and how she spoke to our hearts. You still hold the record in our books, Jennifer! I'm so jealous that she met her! Common bonds abound on the trail! So, mother and son are thru hiking together this year and hope to eventually triple crown together, as well. Woo-hoo!! Love it!

Slam came bouncing into camp about 45 minutes after I arrived. I thought I had lost her! We embraced like long lost sisters (even though we have seen each other mere hours before lol) and pitched our tents. I built a small fire for some quick warmth before the rain hit and we shared delightful conversation with Kimberly and her son, Exterminator (apparently, he fears no shelter mouse!) Spirits are high here at Grassy Gap!

The first raindrops started plopping through the trees and we scrambled to our tents in the nick of time. A downpour! Warm and dry in my tent (Yay rainfly!). Catching up on phone calls, tweaking my itinerary and reflecting on the day. I felt strong today. My heart, lungs and muscles are rising to the challenge. Thriving with all this fresh air and hard work. Couldn't. Be. Happier. Almost delirious with joy because I'm doing it. I thought alcoholism had killed my dream forever. I remember the days without hope. Without passion or dreams. Resigning myself to death. And even when I gave up drink and was able to "function", thinking it was too late for me. That I had ruined any chance I had to get out here and certainly didn't deserve it in the first place. But here I am. Grace abounds. I'm humbled that I have this opportunity and so much support. It boggles my mind, truly. Hope is beginning to stir somewhere in my inner child's heart. A foreign feeling, and somewhat terrifying. But there, nonetheless. The trail is bringing me back to life. Resurrecting confidence, playfulness, courage. Daring me to be me. The old me. The real me. What an unexpected and glorious gift.

Signing off for now! Hope to check in from Stecoah Gap tomorrow! Happy Trails!

Side note- my new trail name is *drumroll* Tink Tank. My Disney obsession has followed me here and married my "put-your-head-down-and-get-it-done attitude. It fits, I suppose.

April 21, 2016

Woke around 7am to more rain. Slam packed up and joined me and my lazy bones in my tent for breakfast before heading out. The next shelter was 4 miles away and we decided to hurry there and make a plan. My new rain jacket I shelled out some big bucks for was NOT waterproof. I found myself having to take breaks from using my trekking poles in order to let the water pooled at my elbows run out. Very strange sensation. But I was too cold to change and wanted to keep moving, so I went with it. Passed several hikers holed up in their tents and longed to join them in their coziness.

The rain did make the hike stunningly beautiful. Loads of rhododendron and mossy boulders were somehow more magical and mysterious when laced with fog and glistening with rainwater. That didn't quell the disappointment I felt, however, when time after time I would think I was summiting, only to realize the trail was STILL ascending to what felt like a phantom peak. Word at the packed shelter when I finally arrived was that everybody had experienced this "how am I not there yet?!" phenomenon. Must have been the dampness affecting our calculations...

I quickly changed into warm, dry clothing and prepared a cup of coffee, enjoying the cheerful banter of the twelve or so other hikers taking a respite from the rain. I had decided to just chalk it up as a loss and stay put for the night, but impulsively decided to give Donna (the fabulous lady who runs the Cabin in the Woods hostel where my next mail drop was waiting) a call to explore options. All the hotels and hostels were booked up in town, but I thought I MIGHT be able to swing by and at least grab my waiting parcel. Before I knew it, Slam and I were headed 7 miles down the trail to Stecoah Gap, where Donna was waiting to pick us up and take us to her HOME, where she had room for us! Astounding really, all this kindness. Hot showers, clean clothes and BBQ sandwiches were just what the doctor ordered. What generosity and trust! Thank you, Donna!

My maildrop was exactly what I needed to make the push through the Smokies. The last of my freeze-dried meals and tons of Probars!!! I love freeze-dried because I can carry more days' worth of food and don't have to resupply as often.

Planning to camp outside of Fontana tomorrow and head into the Great Smokies on Sunday! So stoked to see this park as a thru hiker and not just a weekend visitor!

Today was tough. At one point, both Slam and I were laying in a heap together after falling on SLIPPERY rocks, laughing our heads off. I proceeded to fall twice more. Obviously, I didn't learn my lesson the first time! No harm done, fortunately, and it WAS entertaining....

The rain cleared briefly. Just enough so that the hike to Stecoah was sunny for the last few miles, then started back with a vengeance, literally as we stepped through Donna's door. Trail angel indeed!

So tired. So sore. Still waiting for my "hiker appetite" to kick in. Still wouldn't have it any other way. Happy trails!

April 22, 2016

Woke up sick and grumpy. Poor Slam....Got packed up and hit the trail at 10:30, stiff, sore and cold. I hadn't studied my elevation profile for the day and maybe that was a good thing, cause that first climb was WICKED. "Jacob's Ladder", they call it. I FELT like I was climbing all the way to heaven! I stopped for lunch at the shelter at the summit and had a nice chat with Trek. He's interested in helping gluten free/vegan hikers after he completes his hike, so be looking out for that in the years to come!

I couldn't stay grumpy for long. Not with all the beauty around me. I swear the forest had put on her finest perfume today. It was glorious. Rays of bright sunshine shone down through budding branches to douse carpets of wildflowers. Birds were frolicking and sharing what had to be good news with one another, their songs were so cheerful. Puffy white clouds decorated a perfectly blue sky. Pretty soon my heart was singing, too.

The Fontana Shelter is nice! With showers! (Even though I did not use them. Two days in a row with a shower seemed to be breaking the rules...) I pitched my tent near the shelter and headed to the firepit to prepare my dinner and discovered s'mores! Thanks Haiku!! I feel honored to be tenting right beside Special K. A 14-year-old female thru hiker! Geez these girls are inspiring! I am giddy that she is hanging her food on MY bear bag line. Lol. It's the small things out here!

Did some serious stretching last night and felt great today. Still a little nervous about developing shin splints in my left leg, but I think it's loosening up and getting stronger. Will continue to stretch and force myself to slow down on the downhills! Tomorrow I enter the Smokies! So excited! Not so much about the crowds, but what else can you expect in the most visited national park in the country?! Hiked solo today. And boy, did I need it! Found my rhythm. Finally. With a little help from my friends Salt-N-Pepa urging me to push it. Push it real good.

Tomorrow, I start attempting twenty mile days. Hopefully, having to swing down into Fontana in the morning for fuel doesn't cut into my hiking time too much. Not sweating it. PLENTY of time to make up miles! So, my permit is printed and ready, I have eight days of food to get me to Erwin and my friend is going to slack pack me for a short section here in a few days! I'm ready to go! Still can't get over everyone's support and generosity! Thank you! #livingthedream!

April 23, 2016

Well, apparently my mathematical skills are lacking (not that they were ever strong), because that was not a twenty-mile day. It surely FELT like it! Woke up feeling under the weather again and hoped I could drink enough water and take enough vitamin C to ward off anything that might want to take me down. Packed up, ate some breakfast with the crew and hit the ground...hobbling. It usually takes me a few miles to really get going, but today was a struggle. The Fontana Dam was really something to see, and I am so against dams! Check out the film DamNation if you are curious why! Hiked hard for three hours, parked next to a tree and ate a HUGE lunch. This put a little pep in my step, and I caught up to Slam, doctoring a blister and chatting with Carl, the Ridgerunner. He checked my permit and gave us some info on what to expect further down the trail, painting a picture in my head of an easy, gentle downward slope for the remaining 11 miles of our hike. Lol, he obviously has a different idea of what "easy" means. The hike was mostly uphill, which meant Slam experienced interruptions in my telling of "The Magician's Nephew" (Lewis), because I get too winded trying to sweat it out up the hills at her pace AND maintain a steady stream of speech. We would get about two minutes into a downhill and I would hear, "So what happened next?". Made it pass quickly! In return, she told me a harrowing tale from her PCT days, which included a dangerous creek crossing where she suffered a dunking and almost lost her boots, a severe lightning storm and camping with questionable characters. Superbly entertaining!

The Smokies smell like home and the Hackberry trees look like it. It's nice. The trail here is more like a ditch cutting through the terrain from all the foot traffic. Gnarled trees, some married to ancient boulders and most not even budding yet, remind me of a Tim Burton film and create an excellent juxtaposition for the delicate flowers that COVER the forest floor. Seriously, it's stunning. As far as you can see, in every direction, it's blue, white, yellow and pink beauties rising from a lush, green carpet to flutter carefree in the breeze. Ever protected by sleeping giants which seem to be taking their time waking from their slumber this year.

Ate SO much today. This must be the beginning of my "hiker appetite". Even when I had just eaten, I would find myself thinking about what I would eat next. Good thing I'm lugging around all this food! And it's nice to eat my pack weight. I believe I'm still just under thirty pounds with seven days of food tucked in tight. Not bad! (My legs beg to differ...). I can tell I am getting stronger, though. When I walk anywhere without my pack, I stand taller and walk stronger than I have in months. Legs are still protesting, though. A zero day on the 28th cannot get here soon enough! Still one or two days behind on my challenging schedule. Still not sweating it.

I am looking forward to some great views tomorrow! I can see glimpses of majestic and hazy mountaintops on the horizon through scraggly branches and am looking forward to a clear view. The Spence Field shelter is in fairy land. Just so you know. I felt like Gretel approaching the witch's abode. Fortunately, without her sense of impending doom. Such a rich and varied landscape. Was able to tent tonight, which was probably a good thing, because three mice were spotted before we had even finished dinner! One even climbed on Slam. I was impressed she could move that fast after today's hike! Vegan curried lentils and veggies HIT THE SPOT for dinner tonight. Jack tried some (he's vegan) and agreed it was delicious. I envied my neighbors nightcap of hot cocoa. Might need to implement that into my routine. Fetched another liter of water to chug before sleep and hit the sack. 9:30pm. My earliest turn in yet, and STILL after "hiker midnight" (9pm). Honestly though, I may or may not have been dozing while hiking those last few miles. I was exhausted today. I almost fell asleep changing in my tent before dinner! But my hunger was too insistent to let me sleep and I forced myself up to the campfire to listen to my fellow hiker's friendly banter as I prepared and consumed my meal. Love my new "family". So much laughter, tolerance and kindness. Across the board.

So, even after a really tough day of hills, sickness and pain, I lay in my tent, listening to the owls and coyotes, and can't help smiling. Which, incidentally, hurts my chapped lips. Oh well. The smile in my heart doesn't hurt at all.

Sweet Dreams and Happy Trails!

April 24, 2016

Cell service has been spotty 'round here parts, so unable to update journal two days in a row! Scribbling this down in the "notes" section of my phone tonight, in hopes I can upload in the morning.

Two twenties in a row! Must be getting my "legs" because I feel great! Yesterday (the 25th) was a long day. Still feeling really congested as I left the Spence Field Shelter around 9:30am. Took a while to get out of camp because I decided, last minute, to download an audiobook. Slam and Jack hit the trail at about 8:30am, so I knew I wouldn't be seeing any more of them until evening. Loved hiking alone. The wind and clouds made me feel like I was in Tolkien's world today. Took lunch a mere six miles down the trail at the Derrick Knob Shelter, which has an excellent water source, only it's at the bottom of a VERY steep hill. So, I decided to take my food bag down to the source and eat nearby to avoid making the climb twice. Once down, I realized that one, I had forgotten my spoon and two, there was actually another, less steep trail just to the left of the source. Well done, Les. The next five hours were spent booking it. I had checked my guidebook while eating and realized that included in today's hike was the summit of Clingmans's Dome (6667 ft.) and I still had fourteen miles to my chosen shelter. Yikes! Jules (from Germany and 65 years old) was my cheerleader today. I passed her twice and she was so encouraging! What a lady!

Nice, spotty views from Silers Bald! I was passing the Double Spring Shelter, about to begin my Clingmans's ascent, feeling discouraged and exhausted, when a hiker waylaid me to offer a freshly baked chocolate chip cookie. Yes, please! I am convinced it was that cookie that got me up that mountain! Passed a lovely gentleman day hiker on top of Mt. Buckley who was a local and gave me some nice trail info and extra encouragement. Made the last push to the summit and headed up the Star Wars-esque observation deck. WOW. Totally worth it! Lots of day hikers (who carefully avoided eye contact with me) enjoying the view. I approached the one I gauged to be the most receptive and politely inquired if he would be willing to take a somewhat goofy picture of me. Of course, he agreed. I proceeded to lay face-down on the observation deck floor, pack and all, and said "cheese". This drew smiles from all and I noticed 2 or 3 others snapping photos of me with their personal cameras. I could imagine what they were thinking. Just doing my part to keep the "crazy, dirty thru-hiker" stereotype alive! I thanked my photographer, snapped a few panoramic photos and hit the trail to tackle the remaining four miles to the Mt. Collins Shelter. Such a lovely stretch of trail. Mossy cedar everywhere! The trail was mostly loose stone and step downs, soggy and steep. One last climb and I made it to the shelter right at dusk. It was full (yay!), which allowed me to camp, cowboy style again, with Slam and Endless, Slam's new friend. Quickly made some potatoes and ate while Endless read a chapter of White Fang to us. Perfect ending to a long day in the woods.

April 25, 2016

Woke at 6:30am after a solid night's sleep and hit the trail by 7am, busting it five miles up the trail to Newfound Gap. And Trail Magic. As soon as I hit the gap parking lot, I was waved over to a veritable feast by two kind ladies from Sevierville Baptist Church. I consumed no less than one apple, one orange, one banana, a yogurt cup, granola bar, six Oreo's and three mini snickers. Best. Breakfast. Ever. I connected on Facebook with one of the ladies and plan on sending her ministry team a box of goodies from Omaha once I complete the trail. The next hiker in was from Knoxville and we discovered that he runs in the same climbing circle as my youngest brother, who attends university there. Small world! Caught the shuttle into Gatlinburg to pick up stove fuel and batteries for my headlamp, then back up to the gap to keep hiking. So. Many. Tourists. Everywhere. We encountered a small traffic jam on the way back up and were joking that somebody must have seen Yogi the Bear and were delighted to discover we were (mostly) correct! A mama black bear and her two adorable cubs were parked right by the road! Exciting! My first bear sighting! The whole thing was certainly tamer than I had imagined it would be. No coming around the corner on the trail and coming face to face with a bear, for sure! So far, I have seen four deer, three bears, two turkeys and countless squirrels and chipmunks. Two chipmunks were playing tag in the branches above me for a bit on the trail today. That put a little bounce in my step and smile on my face.

The remaining fifteen miles of my hike started out rough. I must have been dehydrated, because I was having thoughts of quitting (!?). Right at that moment my dad called me (I happened to have service!) and I made it about two minutes before starting to cry. "It's so hard", I sniffled into my phone. "Well, I know you have to climb up one side of the mountain before you can go down the other side", was all he said. I wanted to petulantly point out that I was well aware of this, since it was all I had been doing for two weeks straight! But I knew what he meant.

I want this so bad. All the planning and hoping and dreaming. I can't give up just because the "mountain" I've chosen to go over is not as fun or as easy to climb as I thought, initially. I must put in the dirty, tough, grunt work now if I want to reap the rewards waiting on the other side. What a perfect reminder and word of encouragement. Preach, dad! That phone call and the bear sighting were just the push I needed! Funny how things keep working out that way. The Lord indeed steadies my feet as I walk. I stumbled across this promise in the Good Book the night before my hike and it has become my mantra.

Starting to catch up to a lot of hikers who started well before me and who somehow know of Slam and me. Stopped at the Groundhog Creek Shelter for lunch and was asked immediately if I was "that chick trying to do it in 100 days". Lol. Now I MUST do it. That, and I already have my plane ticket purchased.

Saw only one other hiker for the rest of the day. Stomach started acting up with about five miles to go, requiring frequent stops and toilet paper rationing. I will drink no more sodas while hiking! Began sprinkling on me with about four miles to go. Didn't mess with rain gear, just covered my pack and kept moving. I had opted not to walk the half mile down to the Peck's Corner Shelter for water earlier and soon regretted it. I was SO thirsty and drained. I thought I had misjudged the distance I had remaining when the trail headed upwards again when I thought it should be going downhill to the shelter. This led me to believe I had yet ANOTHER uphill climb before I reached me destination. I had just readied my heart for what I was sure was going to be a brutal climb with no water, when I rounded the corner and there it was! Shelter! I could have cried. So, I had made it to the Tri-corner Knob Shelter before dark! I quickly set up my tent, changed out my damp clothes, chugged a liter of water and joined the other hikers at the fire for dinner. This bunch is silly and almost had me snorting Ramen out of my nose.

Another long day tomorrow but, without any resupply needs, I should be able to have a nice, leisurely hike. Lots of pictures, I hope! Farewell for now!

April 26, 2016

Sitting at the Standing Bear Hostel with Endless and Tabasco, talking trail. Endless is from Massachusetts and is a fireman. His accent is ridiculous. He hiked the PCT last year! Tabasco is from Oklahoma and hiked the AT last year. He loved it so much, he's back for more! I mentioned that I have never been to the New England area and they both flipped and said I was in for a treat, agreeing that the Smokies have nothing on the Whites. So stoked for that part of the journey! Tabasco told a touching table about another hiker and I teared up. We bonded in that moment. The magic of the trail brings us all together.

I slept in today (27th), not sure if I was going to attempt my full twenty miles, finally breaking camp around 11:00am. Six section hikers were just arriving at the shelter for lunch, and we chatted for a bit. I told them my story of why I was thru-hiking and they thanked me and said they were encouraged which, in turn, encouraged me!

The hike today was mostly gentle ups and downs, and I ate up ground. Stopped at Cosby Knob Shelter for lunch and met two other female thru-hikers from Nashville! Yee-haw! Apparently, there is a bear that frequents this shelter daily looking for food. Signs are everywhere. I found myself hoping it would show up while I was there...probably not the wisest dream to dream.

An hour into my remaining hike it started POURING. I quickly ripped a head and arm holes in the trash bag I had picked up for this very purpose, donning it as quickly as I could. Makeshift poncho. No rain outfit would be complete without a grocery bag rain bonnet, so I threw that over my head as well! I must have looked incredible. The downpour lasted about an hour, but I was warm and dry. The rain released wonderful aromas and made the freshly budding foliage fairly glow green. I couldn't wipe the smile off my face or help singing aloud. Hiking in the rain is the best! (Ask me my opinion on this again, tomorrow. Forecast is calling for rain all day!)

I decided to bypass the Davenport Shelter and head the extra three miles down trail to the Standing Bear Farm Hostel because I was OUT of toilet paper (thanks to yesterday's fun times). I walked in, still wearing my trash bag, around 8pm and was able to quickly pitch my tent in a large nearby field. Managed this well in the rain. I was glad I wasn't using a new, unfamiliar tent, which surely would have slowed me down and put me in even more of a damp situation. I nabbed some hot cocoa packets in addition to toilet paper and an ACTUAL rain bonnet from the hostel "store" and proceeded to satisfy my days long hot chocolate craving! Hit the spot! Borrowed "Heidi" from the bookshelf and am now warm, dry and cozy in my tent, reading and looking forward to another great day on the trail. There is allegedly some bangin' trail magic at Brown's Gap and I can't wait to see if the stories of steak and lobster are true! So, either a nine-mile hike to Brown's, or a twenty to Lemon Gap. Either way, I can't wait to experience whatever the trail has in store for me tomorrow!

April 27, 2016

Ahhhhhhh. My feet are rejoicing! No pack and no tramping around today! Hopefully, I can stretch out all the soreness and kinks! I am trading in my Keen boots for my lighter Salomon trail runners, ditching my fleece pants and gloves and picking up my North Face raincoat. Hopefully, these changes are for the better. Was able to dry out all my gear and wash all my STINKY laundry, resupply for four days of breakfast and lunch and organize and clean my pack. Feeling good! The plan is to slack pack into Hot Springs tomorrow and, depending on the fire situation (about 16 miles of trail north of Hot Springs has been closed due to a forest fire), hike on a few miles from there. Finally nailing down my food routine. Hot chocolate, instant coffee and oatmeal for breakfast. Nut and berry trail mix with m&m's, fiber fruit chews and sometimes ramen for lunch. Pasta sides, instant potatoes or freeze-dried meals for dinner. Not the MOST nutritional diet, but grabbing fruits and veggies to supplement when I can, taking a daily multivitamin and drinking ALOT of water, so hopefully I can power on and not develop scurvy or something else disturbingly farfetched.

Might need to pick up insoles for my runners, so hopefully there is an outfitter nearby! So now, while I have the chance, I'm shaving ounces from my pack weight and looking over my map. I'm fully submerged, it appears, in trail life. Completely unconcerned by anything except my pack (my life!), food, water and my physical condition. With so few things to concern myself with, I find I am that much more grateful for the little things. Well, really the big things all along. The richness of nature, the joy of human companionship, the delight of discovering absurd capabilities. And you should check the stars out here! Totally rad.

April 28, 2016

Decided to wait one day in Hot Springs until the trail reopens tomorrow, instead of shuttling around the fire this morning and coming back later to complete the missed miles. You can see the charred patches on the mountains surrounding the town of Hot Springs and it's crazy to think how close it was. Sitting here at the Laughing Heart Hostel under a Tulip Poplar and a Hackberry, gazing up at the remains of some powerful nature stuff. Hundreds of acres burned and word on the street is that it was man made. Lots of crazy stories running around the trail community of how it started. Pretty entertaining.

The hike from Max Patch to Hot Springs was rough. Ended up hiking about two hours after dark, my feet totally getting eaten alive by my trail runners. But what I did see was lovely. Lots of rain, so the aromas were incredible. Everything was so lush and green with lots of rhododendron tunnels weaving up and down, in and out of the mist wreathed peaks. Felt very homey and welcoming. Once darkness fell, I was led to the town of Hot Springs by the music drifting up from a festival in full swing. Really cool feeling, to walk in from the woods, greeted by music echoing around you.

I've been eating like CRAZY. So fun! It's dinner and sleep action for me! So tired and relaxed, ready for good sleep and a good hike tomorrow. I miss the trail!

April 29, 2016

Whew. What a day. The hostel was stirring to life when I rose at 6:30am this morning. Folks waiting for the shower, grabbing coffee, packing up and munching on breakfast. All cheerful and so ready to hit the newly opened trail! Made a quick exit and beat the stampede. Only ran into a few hikers today. Mostly Lionheart, this rad girl from Maine.

Hiking through the burn area was surreal. Saw a few logs still smoldering and ran into the sheriff and some fire fighters at the tail end of the burn zone. Otherwise, it was quiet, with little sign of animal life, save a few birds and snakes. The trail was untouched by flame, making it obvious that the fire was controlled/contained here. Strange to walk between stretches of scorched earth on fair ground. The flames did not reach too high above the ground from what I could see, but green rhododendron tunnels became golden ones and wildflowers were replaced with a bare forest floor.

Struggled with some knee pain later in the day and decided to only go a few miles past the Little Laurel Shelter, to Jones Meadow. It was sprinkling by the time I arrived in the general location and lack of water forced me to push on another half mile or so. I quickly got my tent set up before the rain came POURING down! But I was warm and dry and cozy, and the rain suits me. Got a little scare when lightning hit nearby several times. I'm not on a summit, but I am near the top, in the clouds, of Camp Creek Bald. Hearing the thunder rumble from inside a cloud is tops! Did have thoughts of falling trees. Maybe got goosebumps. It was pretty thrilling for a city girl like me.

Snuck out to hang my bear bag during a slight break in the rain and am now all tucked in, alone in my meadow, listening to the rain drumming on my (performing) rainfly and wondering what I did to deserve this much fun. Yes, it hurts. I've (almost) accepted the fact that I won't be hiking pain free. Just pushing through it. Letting my body absorb the pressure and adjust. Not pushing too hard. Always listening for that sharp pain to let me know something's not right. But knowing that my body is just the vehicle, and to not forget to let my soul enjoy this treat of nature. It truly is the Appalachian SCENIC Trail!

April 30, 2016

May showers bring June flowers? Rained until about 3pm today. Packed up in the rain. Tent (and almost everything else) was soaking by the time I was through, but it kept me dry all night, therefore I was happily dry during these shenanigans. Good day for hiking. Mostly mud gazing. Trail was heck-a slick. It was foggy, too, which meant you weren't missing any views while trying to step down, over, around, under(?!) slippery boulders or trying to avoid the crick running down the middle of the trail. Stopped at both the Jerry Cabin Shelter and the Flint Mountain Shelter to eat and water up. Met Lionhearted and D-3 both times so we chatted and relaxed together. Cheerfully complaining about the damp conditions. We were all muddy, muddy, muddy and having an absolute blast. The last 9 miles were sunny and beautiful. My leg was really loosening up and I was staying fueled and hydrated, so I felt good about picking up the pace and stretching out. Lots of pasture walks today. Signs to shoo dogs away if they follow you because they are family pets and they follow hikers and never return. Bummer. Made it to the Hogback Ridge Shelter around 6pm and decided to call it a day and head out early the next morning for Erwin.

Pebbles, GI Joe, Lionheart, D-3, Jack, James, Dueces and I are joking around and in high spirits. Pebbles is sixteen! Meal finished, stretching complete, bear bag hung, constellation lesson adjourned (thanks James!) and I'm ready to crawl into my sleeping bag. I'm staying in the shelter while my tent (pitched nearby) dries out (totally soaked!). We saw one mouse at 7:21pm, so we know to expect them. It's fun creepy. James told us all about his experiences on the Florida trail at dinner tonight, so mice seem like the little leagues now. Sweet Dreams!

May 4, 2016

Not a drop of rain fell on me yesterday, but it was COLD. Broke camp just before 6am to start my longest hike yet. Didn't even bother with my hiking clothes, just wore my long johns for a couple hours until I warmed up a bit. Pack was super light, since I had eaten ALL my food and it felt great! Pretty tough hike. LOTS of up-down, up-down. The sunrise was misty and glorious. Gliding through dew-soaked pastures, warmed by the sun piercing through the heavy clouds resting on the mountaintops, thinking that it just doesn't get better than this. Breaks were short today in order to ward off the chill. Lionheart, Deuces, GI Joe and I shivering and wolfing down our lunches and discussing various aches and pains. The camaraderie is so encouraging and uplifting. The playing field is just so leveled out here and it makes understanding and accepting one another that much easier. The vegetation was lush, the trail edges laced with bright green moss, ferns and, of course, rhododendron. Almost got blown over while crossing one of the balds. So windy! As I passed by the No Business Knob shelter 20 miles into my hike, only to continue another 8 miles to Erwin, I was literally cheered on by my friends. Jack, GI Joe and Lionheart whooped and hollered and offered encouraging words, urging me on. I needed it! The Advil had worn off and I was struggling to walk normally and not hobble. My feet ached and my Achilles felt so tight. I was hungry, but I had attempted a strange muffin lunch in my Jetboil, and it was full of purple, crusty paste and I didn't feel like washing it out in order to cook my last item of food, a freeze dried fajita mix. So, I just drank extra water and pushed on, knowing food was just a few miles down the trail. It was grueling, not going to lie. Finally, I popped out of the woods into Erwin, TN., greeted by the mighty Nolichucky. I texted my good friend, Kasey, who grew up in Erwin, and she came to pick me up right at the trailhead! What a treat! I told her, since I wasn't ever able to drive out and visit her, I had just quit my job and WALKED to her. We got a good chuckle out of that one. First stop: milkshake. Second stop: Walmart to resupply. Then, a tour of Erwin (such a cute, nice town) and on to Kasey's parents' house, where I was showered with affection, allowed to do laundry and dry out my tent. I asked Kasey if there was anything I could do for her and she said, "Take a shower." Lol, I don't even smell myself anymore! Woke up this morning to discover that the pup had cuddled with me during the night! So now I'm wrapping up laundry, updating my journal and getting my food bag organized and stocked. Hiking out in a few hours for a short day to the shelter about 5 miles out. So grateful for the kindness of others. It has been so incredible to be on the receiving end of such generosity! Can't wait to get back in the woods, carrying the warmth of good company in my heart. Happy trails!

May 6, 2016

Made it to the Curley Maple Gap Shelter last night at about 7:30 or 8pm. The 4.5-mile hike was excellent. Very jungle-y. Four nice footbridges to cross and the sound of rushing cricks could be heard the whole walk. I wasn't paying attention at one point and missed a switchback, plunging me up a dry creek bed and into a mess of a "trail". Halfway over my third huge tree (and countless other branches, vines, etc.) I paused and reconsidered. Obviously, I was not in the right spot. This suddenly became clear. Backtracking 75 or so yards, I snorted at my blindness. The trail was CLEARLY marked. Reminding me, again, to stay on my toes. This trail might be well-worn and clearly blazed, but it is not messing around. I was last to the shelter, where almost everyone was already in their bags. I quickly got settled and ate quietly, as not to disturb the others. I probably did, though, as it was raining and I was stuck cooking and eating five feet from their heads. I headed over to the small but hot fire to read in the rain (cell phone in a "touch-screen-friendly" Ziplock) and warm my hands near the embers. A nice, quiet night by which to ease back into trail life.

Thought about getting up before 5am when I awoke but am always wary of disturbing others when in shelters, and I was so warm.... ended up getting up at 7:30am, hiked out at 8:30-8:45am. Hike was suuuper foggy today. Not a lot of steady rainfall, but I wore my full rain gear all day long. It was chilly, as well. Just had to keep moving, really. I was kicking myself for ditching my gloves three days before! Unaka mountain was crazy! Not only is it a dense spruce forest for most of its upper elevation, but it was foggy, snow-covered and the trail was soggy. And by soggy, I mean it was a creek. Literally. I never gave up trying to keep my feet dry, even after they were beyond soaked. I nearly fell so many times and it was real slow going. I began to question if my 22-mile day was going to be possible. The trail finally dried up and a few miles later, stopped at Cherry Gap Shelter for a hot lunch Lionheart and GI Joe were in their bags, warming up, when I pulled up. We were all three pushing on the extra 9 miles to the Clyde Smith Shelter. I wished them happy trails right as I dug into my ramen. Soon afterward, Roc Solid pulled up. He was staying there for the night, so I told him whom he could probably expect to join him. We had a nice, inspiring conversation before I bid him adieu. It cleared up a little bit for the second half of the hike, but was still pretty chilly. Slam happened to call me while my phone wasn't in airplane mode, and we discovered that she was ten miles behind me. We expect her to catch up in 2-3 days. I miss her!

The trail made me proud to be from Tennessee today. Rolling pastures, magnificent forests, demanding elevation changes, wild weather, lush foliage. What a thrill.

Rolled into the shelter at about 7:30pm. It was full, so I quickly pitched my tent in the spattering rain. Everything is dry and I'm cozy, with bear bag hung* and everything! So sleepy and hoping for an early start tomorrow. Haven't nailed down an itinerary, but I'm hoping to put in some solid miles. Sweet dreams from Clyde Smith Shelter!

* really, this shouldn't even count as a bear bag hang. It's pitiful. I gave up and now it probably would be better if I didn't even hang it at all. Oh well, there's always next time....

May 7, 2016

Roan Mountain was intense! Good thing there was trail magic right before we began our ascent! Thanks to Waves, who thru-hiked last year, we had waffles, coffee, banana pudding, brownies, chips, cookies, soda, avocados, oranges, everything! Amazing! The perfect fuel for four straight miles of uphill, gaining 2100ft. The trail was super soggy again today. A creek at some parts, deep mud at some and rocks/roots for the rest-when it wasn't a boulder scramble. I am exhausted just thinking about it. Saw lots of day hikers at Carver's Gap, it being a Saturday and all. Weather was fine, indeed. A bit blustery, but that's what you want on top of the balds! And the view! Incredible! The earth just rippled away beneath us, as far as you could see. No photo I took did it justice.

Decided to push on about six miles past the Overmountain Shelter (an old, converted barn) to Doll Flats, right on the NC/TN border, to camp. And boy, was that rough. Little Hump Mountain and Hump Mountain stood in my way. Both balds and the wind gusting at 50mph. It blew me over once. Just sat me down on the side of the trail furrow. Every muscle in my body was straining against it for three miles. I was drained. Luckily, the next two miles were downhill, covered and had dry patches! Pulled up to Doll Flats around 7:15pm, pitched my tent and began to prepare my meal by the fire with some friendly section hikers when, of course, it started raining. Scarfed down my meal, hung my bear bag and dove into my tent. Apparently, there is a big storm headed our way tonight, so I grabbed some huge rocks, dragged a smallish log over and made some tent fortifications. I've been using twigs as stakes for a couple days now (lost my set?) and I hope they prove reliable tonight. I can feel it getting colder and hear the wind and rain picking up, so I think I'll take this time to say goodnight and snuggle in nice and tight! Happy Trails!

May 8, 2016

Slept in a tad this morning. Awoke at 7:30am, grabbed my bear bag and crawled back into my tent for hot coffee and Taylor Swift to pump me up for what certainly appeared to be another day of hiking in cruddy weather. I was packing up my tent, surprised to see Jack (London)'s tent still up (he usually breaks camp around 5 or 6am), when all of a sudden, he comes busting out, all sleepy-eyed and bewildered, asking for the time. Guess he overslept, too. Pretty amusing. Walked out at just before 9am, looking forward to a pancake breakfast in Elk Lodge, NC, just four miles up the trail. I needed batteries for my headlamp, so I had decided to hitch down and grab a short stack while I was at it. Reached the road and began the 2.4 mile walk into town, realizing pretty quickly that this wasn't going to be easy. At least thirty cars passed me! I had resigned myself to the walk, when a little Subaru hatchback pulled over about 100 yards up the road. I dared to hope. Sure enough, a young lady hopped out and asked me if I needed a ride! "Yeesss!", I cried gratefully and hopped in. She asked if I was a hiker and got excited when I confirmed that I was, indeed, a thru-hiker. She confessed that she had passed me earlier but was about to wet her pants and had kept driving. She quickly decided to come back and get me, though, bearing a newly purchased ice-cold bottle of water for me! I explained that I was stopping for breakfast, and I asked her if I could buy her a coffee or something and she laughed and told me she was totally going to ask to join me, but she didn't want to creep me out! So we sat and chatted (her best friend is planning a thru-hike!) for a while, me answering questions about my hike and asking her questions about grad school and her writing. She had texted her friend about me and instantly received a bombardment of questions she was supposed to ask me, followed by a screenshot of my trail journal to verify my identity! Lol. It was amazing. Kaitlyn then proceeded to drive me to the Dollar General and back to the trailhead!

Truly a Godsend! We exchanged numbers and parted ways. Thank you, Kaitlyn and good luck Sarah!

Hit the trail again, feeling super sluggish. Pretty soon I found my stride and hoofed it another 12 miles before it started raining. As I was waterproofing my gear, Elf came up behind me and we hiked the last mile to the Vango Hostel together. Stopping for a photo op at the "bench, with view". Somebody carried a nice park bench all the way up and plopped it in just the right spot for a perfect view of Little Hump and Hump Mountains. Absolutely perfect. Rain shut off after a few minutes and we made our way down a side trail to the hostel, tucked into the side of a mountain in the middle of nowhere. The boundary line for the National Forest is five feet away from his back porch. Scotty, the proprietor, was great! Elf and I decided to bunk in the $5 bunkhouse and after pizza and good conversation on the back porch with a hummingbird visitor, I am now tucked in all cozy, being kept in stitches by Elf's stories. Hilarious. Satellite WI-FI is out for the night, so I'll have to post in the morning! Sweet Dreams!

May 9, 2016

Elf and I hadn't even made it back to the trail before we ran into Slam! Yippee! #reunion! Ended up hiking together and meeting up with two others along the way. My largest hiking group yet! We played the "monster game" for about two hours straight. Taking turns thinking of monsters/villains and having the others guess what it was. Like "20 Questions", but without the limit of 20 questions. Very entertaining. Our "monsters" included Pikachu, Professor Moriarty and the Molemen. I was impressed by the variety.

It was amazing how the miles seemed to fly by with company, after three days of solo hiking. Passed through another burn area, which we later learned had been arson. The contrast between the lush, green views and the charred ground beside the trail was more pronounced, it seemed, than it had been back in Hot Springs. There were a couple of steep climbs, but, for the most part, the trail was downhill. And dry! Easy, breezy! The rhododendron is budding and will soon bloom. Can't wait!

Hiked about twelve miles to Dennis Cove Road, where we intended to stay at Kincora Hostel, run by Bob People's. Our arrival here put a pause to my telling of "The Silver Chair" (Lewis), which was just getting interesting. Now, Elf AND Slam are asking for the continuance of the story as soon as we hit a downhill. It's good, wholesome fun.

We quickly dropped our packs on bunks to claim them and rushed back outside to cram into Bob's truck with nine other hikers for the harrowing descent into Hampton, TN. Several miles of dangerously steep, curvy (sometimes one lane) highway and lots of laughs at Bob's extremely witty humor later, we pulled into Brown's Grocery and Feed Store. Honestly, I wasn't sure whether I should use the grocer or the feed store. Pretty sure I could have used a salt lick. Ended up getting muffin mix for muffins and eggs, peppers and onion for an omelet in which to use the Morel mushroom I found! Delicious! And the cat smell in the hostel was temporarily masked by a delightful aroma of wild blueberry muffins. Everyone was a winner!

As I sit and listen to the life stories of the hikers with whom I am sharing this journey, I am struck by how much pain and suffering we have collectively shrugged off in order to shoulder our packs and experience a whole new type of pain and suffering. Fighting for each step, enduring physical pain and mental weakness, building grit. And somehow, it's healing. Refreshing for the soul. The weight of the pack we bear physically becoming enough to assuage guilty consciousnesses and disallowing any heaviness of spirit. The glory of the natural world we are "bathing" ourselves in (the Japanese word for "hiking" translates to "forest bathing"!) washing the past away. As our physical bodies become more capable of load bearing, so do our minds and hearts become more capable. More capacious. More willing to extend compassion and demote self. Much more willing to experience joy. To let in peace. Everything we have sacrificed to make this journey is being paid back two-hundred-fold in ways I never dreamed. Making me wonder- was there any sacrifice at all? Or merely a release from burdens we were not aware we were bearing?

A lazy day today. Sitting on the front porch of the hostel, sipping coffee and listening to the trail warriors share their wisdom and experience. Learning things I never thought to think of. Seeds being planted in my heart. A beautiful sunny, breezy day, which the birds seem to be enjoying, too! Anticipating the trail and our eight mile hike today and our forty mile "Damascus Dash" tomorrow. Letting the wonder of it all outshine the logistics. Enjoying the fellowship instead of striving for solitude. Finally, just relaxing. Trusting the journey and, more importantly perhaps, myself.

May 10, 2016

As you know, this morning was lazy. Meant to head out at noon. Ended up hiking out at 1:30pm. It's Elf, Slam and I until we hit Damascus tomorrow and part ways. Slam is interested in Trail Days festivities, while Elf and I are decidedly not. So, she will stay in town for a few days, while Elf and I will press on. I might need to rush a bit, seeing as my next food drop is in Marion and I'm getting low in rations.

Today was great! Stopped at Laurel Falls about two miles into our hike. And it was beautiful. No swimming here, however, as there is a dangerous whirlpool which has drowned several unfortunate swimmers. Ate a quick bite and hit the trail. By this point we had picked up two more hikers. Another large hiking group! So fun. About ten minutes into our ascent of Pond Flats (a gain of about 1700 ft. over 4 miles), Slam and I left the guys behind. We trucked it up that mountain! Sweat dripping, muscles screaming, heart pounding, lungs gasping and nausea threatening. We did it in about an hour. Amazing how she absolutely murders me with her uphill pace! But, then I'm so glad at the end because it's OVER. Elf, claiming to have narrowly escaped death by ascent as well, caught us at the water source near the summit, where we were catching our breath. We proceeded to try and make it the next two miles in under an hour to catch alleged trail magic at Watauga Lake. Of course, on the way we heard a little bit more of "The Silver Chair" (Lewis), it being downhill and all. Puddleglum the Marshwiggle seems to be fan favorite.

We "rumbled" (a stumbling run) into trail magic JUST as they were packing up but, being the true trail angels they are, we were still given sustenance and conversation. Grannie's daughter thru-hiked in 2014, and she "just wants to show some of the love that her daughter was shown". That seems to be a reoccurring theme among these angels. It's mostly folk just paying it forward. Amazing. And, after being out here for just one month, I can understand 100%. I'm already excited by the prospect of providing trail magic to future hikers! I mean, what a kick!

I hope I have the opportunity, nay, the honor, to join these angels' ranks one day.

Sat by the lakeside for about an hour after the magic was gone with a group of about 15 hikers. Chatting, joking around and discussing plans for the coming days. Everyone is STOKED for Trail Days. What an awesome thing!

Slam, Elf and I decided to hoof it back up the trail about a half mile, where we would tent it, while almost everyone else decided to take a hitch offer up and head back to Kincora for the night, shuttling back to the lake in the morning. Our plan is to wake up around 3 or 4am to begin our 40 mile "dash" to Damascus. Gah, I really hope we don't crash and burn. Sooo possible. No sweat, though. Naps ARE an option. Lol.

Elf is wonderful hiking company. Always ready with a joke and positive attitude. So, as I am luckily hiking with him AND Slam, I find myself laughing almost continuously.

Camp was an adventure tonight. It started raining just as we got pitched and we chatted while cooking in our respective tents. Realizing too late that our tent set up was not conducive to chatting (if you kindly recall, it was raining), we were reduced to practically shouting at one another alternate tent arrangements for next time. Somehow, voicing my wishful thinking that the rain would cease in 30-45 minutes so that our tents could dry out before we had to pack them in the morning (forecast calls for more rain at 4am) worked. Because it happened. Exactly 30-45 minutes later the rain stopped. Elf's comment "Well, you're awesome" had me laughing out loud again. We tried three separate times to hang all three bear bags together, resulting in broken branches, slight head injuries, a broken rope, some more laughter (this involved Miss Awesome falling straight on her rear. Hard.) and eventual success. But only after we hung two separate ropes to distribute the weight of our bags. Spirits were high throughout this debacle and, during a pause in the action, we all enthusiastically agreed that the current fun level was extraordinarily high.

While strolling up the small knoll to our tents, we discovered the sky was completely clear and we had an EXCELLENT view of the night sky. A multitude of stars, a pristine crescent moon. We managed to correctly identify The Big Dipper. And that was it. We're quite the group of astronomers. But the lightning bugs were out (the first!), the sky was lighting up with distant lightning and we felt compelled to offer applause. We applauded the stars, the moon, the lightning, the lightning bugs, the nearby whippoorwill and even ourselves (the happy bear bag ending) for such a great night's show. A moment of pure joy. This is so good. The trail is somehow pervaded with goodness. And I'm grateful, so grateful, for my acquaintance with it. My friends, it doesn't get much better than this. Sweet Dreams and Happy Trails!

May 11, 2016

What a whirlwind these past couple of days have been. I am exhausted. So, our plan DID fall apart. Lost Slam at Shady Valley, TN and Elf somewhere after that. Ended up doing 32 miles and parking it for a few hours at the Double Springs Campsite. Stopped in to ask campers about a water source and was directed down the hill (bushwacking) about .25 mile, where I may or may not find water. They pointed out that the shelter was only two miles away. I knew this, but I was THIRSY. So, I dropped my pack, grabbed my Nalgene (&Co) and peered down the holler. I looked back at the camper for reassurance, and he nodded. I set off. So many thorns later I managed to locate a spring! I quickly dug a water bottle size hole in the ground and waited for the pool to fill and dust to settle. So cold and delicious. I trooped my way back up the beast of a hill in triumph. I even think I caught a gleam of approval in the eyes of the camper who had directed me down the godforsaken hill in the first place. I was called over by the friendly section hikers I keep running into and, by the side of their warm, warm fire was slowly convinced that it would be much better for me to just pitch here for a few hours, rather than continuing to hike on in the night. I caved. I pitched, hung my bear bag, ate my dinner (warm, warm fire!), checked for cell service (Nope=No Journal Update), and set my alarm for 4am. It was 11pm.

Woke as planned and quickly hit the trail. Ate a quick breakfast at the shelter down the trail, where people were stirring right as I was packing back up and hiking out. Ten more miles to Damascus! There were mentions of free showers and laundry being available in town, which intrigued me, even though I was hoping to skip through and avoid the Trail Days festivities. I bopped into town around 10am and quickly got through the free shower/laundry line. And who was running it but the same sweet ladies from New-found Gap! What a treat! I was their first repeat, and we were all thrilled to see each other. So, a couple of hours, three cups of coffee, four blueberry muffins and some of the best black bean salsa I've ever had in my life later and I was back on the trail. Deuces is the only other hiker from my group that wants to beat the "Damascus Bubble", and we're both wanting to crush some big miles, so we're kind of sticking together. We started on the same day and keep running into each other, so we must have a similar pace.

Made it to the Saunders Shelter (in the rain!) and managed to squeeze in. So packed with Trail Days peeps. Didn't settle down until late.

Up early and greeted with rain. Lots of it. Deuces and I did a little bit of hesitating before deciding to just go now instead of waiting to see if it cleared. Others began stirring as we packed up. Lots of talk of Trail Days. Again. They didn't understand that we weren't going. That we were hiking on north, instead of south, with them, into Damascus. Even as we hiked out, we were farewelled with "See you in town!" Hilarious.

Whew. Today was rough. Packing some serious food weight and, man, it makes such a difference. I felt like I was back in Georgia! But, let me tell you, it was beyond worth it.

Hiked alone for the middle 14 or so miles of a 19.2-mile day. Did the last four with Deuces and a very cool day hiker, John, who was summiting Mt. Rogers on his way to a wedding in NC. We parted ways (after he gave us water!) and Deuces and I headed a little bit down the trail to the Thomas Knob Shelter. Heard wind of nearby ponies, so we took off to check it out. And, oh. my. goodness. Came around a corner and there they were. A momma and her brand-new foal! Right on the trail. Took a seat and just watched them for like thirty minutes. Pretty soon we were joined by more hikers and pictures were being snapped left and right. The momma got in the spirit of it all and even licked a few hands. Salty, I guess. So cool. Decided to summit Mt. Rogers sans packs and that turned out to be the best decision, ever. There is no view from Virginia's highest peak at 5730 ft, but that hike, with no weight, through what I swear was an enchanted fairy forest, was magical. Dense fir trees, no sound except the wind and the soft squishing of our feet combined with the late afternoon sunbeams streaming through the thick branches, made for a dreamy end to a long day. The view from the shelter was insane. Mountains and mountains and mountains as far as the eye could see. Clear sky, radical sunset and a small fire had us all glad we were right where we were. Cold night, so after a few minutes of stargazing, we all headed to the shelter for a cozy night's sleep. Wow. This is the most magical shelter I've seen so far. Totally recommend a stay here!

Might be resupplying in Troutdale (20 miles), but hopefully, we will make it to the shelter right past it today.

Happy Trails.

May 12, 2016

Made it to the Trimpi Shelter last night around 7:30pm. What a nice shelter. Virginia has had some spiffy shelters so far. This one had a fireplace (which had a fire roaring in it when we pulled up) and two upper bunks. The hike had been a long 25 miles, but included more highland and ponies, so my day had been glorious! Everything is starting to bloom! Rhododendron, Laurel, Lady slippers, Mayapples! Despite the rocky, root-y, muddy, steep, never-ending trail, the sights to be seen are enough to dull any wretchedness.

We shared the shelter with two fathers and their college-age sons. They were super friendly and engaging. They were having a devotion time while we were cooking, which I found comforting and made me think of home. Hit the hay early, nice and toasty with the fire.

Woke up freezing! Did planks and push-ups in my sleeping bag to warm up enough to brave the cold. The plan was to get 11 miles down the trail and hitch into Marion, VA for a resupply. Noticed in the AWOL guide that the Friendship Shelter at the road crossing where we were hitching had showers(!), so that was a possibility, too. The hike was so cold. Never even took my outer shell off. Very windy. But it couldn't take away my pleasure at having the sun shining and a bright, blue sky peeking through the trees.

The man who gave us a ride the six miles down the road mentioned a KFC ALL YOU CAN EAT BUFFET in town, and we promptly agreed to be dropped there. We stayed at least two hours and gorged. Walked up the street to Walmart for fuel and food, then hitched a ride back up to the trailhead. Picked up a few bear evasion tips. Thank you, sir!

Decided to head another eight miles to the next shelter. Lots of windy Roseline trail in this section. Only ran into two-day hikers this afternoon. The trail is so nice and empty. A real treat!

The shelter came up before we knew it and we were so proud of ourselves for doing eighteen miles on a town day! Four other thru-hikers here tonight, so it's business as usual, quiet, with the occasional burst of laughter. Chores are being completed briskly and efficiently, discussing trail life with new friends. I'm looking forward to tenting more often here soon, though.

Who knows what tomorrow brings, haven't even checked! More walking, I suppose.

Good night!

May 13, 2016

Another easy day. I am enjoying the Virginia "rollercoasters". The endless ups and downs, each lasting just long enough to become almost unbearable before tapering off and gently sloping in the opposite direction. Lots of pasture walking and stile climbing (five, I think!) today. Scared a lone cow today. As the trail passes straight through his field, and I'm sure he must know what hikers look like, I was disappointed in his cowardice. Listened to "The Lost World" (Doyle) for most of the day. It made for an imaginative hike.

Pulled into the Knot Maul Shelter around 5:45pm. Quickly knocked out chores and ate a huge dinner. Instant potatoes with a tuna packet thrown in, followed by a Backpacker Pantry s'mores dessert gifted to me a few days ago by section hikers. Joining me here tonight are Deuces, Nala, Sofree, Little Santa, Lucky and a couple of section hikers, Spills and Smoosh.

Haven't seen this many people at a shelter in a few days, signaling the end of Trail Days. Going to try for a 30 miler tomorrow. Need to get moving!

My Big Agnes sleeping pad has developed a slow leak, which I believe to be a nozzle malfunction, so I picked up a $7 foam pad from Walmart and it has worked fine. Keeping me warmer than my inflatable! I will call Big Agnes to see if there is anything they can do for me and my leaky nozzle tomorrow!

There were some picturesque parts of the trail today. At one point, it descended through this lush forest, opening onto a quaint scene of a riverbend with a beautiful farmhouse and well maintained out buildings nearby. The trail was boardwalked through this part and beautiful wildflowers abounded. Even daffodils!

Hoping I won't be too cold for an early start in the morning. Right now, the campfire is keeping me nice and toasty. Pretty satisfied with all my gear right now. I have the perfect number of layers. Only regretting ditching my gloves.

The rain is stop and go right now. Everyone is finishing up dinner and hanging bear bags. This one kid still must pitch his tent and is practically gulping his food. I'm headed to bed early tonight. Pretty worn out despite the low mileage days. My food bag is surprisingly light for being one day out from a resupply. I'm still amazed by how hungry I am. All. The. Time. And I'm still amazed at how bad my shoes smell. I mean, it's horrific. Nothing could prepare you for the rankness.

On that note, I'm off to dreamland!

May 14, 2016

It's only 11am, but I thought I would take advantage of cell service and give a short update.

Hiked out of camp at 5:50am this morning. Everyone else was still fast asleep. Super, super low energy level today. Perhaps the lack of coffee this morning? My left leg was tight and giving me trouble. It was such a mental struggle. I was even thinking how nice it would be to have the option of quitting! What the heck? Made it to the Chestnut Knob Shelter at 10:15am, put on dry clothes and my puffy, started boiling water for coffee and soup and checked the weather. I thought the hill leading up to the shelter was never going to end. After two miles it opened onto balds and despite the very mild rain making for dry feet thus far, the soaking grass lining the narrow trail quickly put an end to that. Cold!

Feel better now that I've eaten and gotten some rest. Every single kind word out here means so much, be it via another hiker or a message from a friend back home. It pushes me.

Going to at least break at the next shelter. Might try to push closer to Bland and tent it. Not sure yet. Okay, here goes!

Happy Trails!

May 17, 2016

Decided to call it a day at the Jenkins Shelter. Just so tired. Going to try and make it 30 miles to Trent's Grocery tomorrow. I can shower, do laundry and tent there for $6. Hopefully, I can charge my battery pack, too. Whole new crowd at the shelter tonight. Cold Taters is the only familiar face. He is trying to finish by August 1st, too!

Lots of funny stories tonight around the campfire. Cold Taters saw his first bear today, so there was a lot of wildlife talk. Apparently, a bear cub scampered right across Tater's path this morning. He said he immediately started hollering because he knew momma was nearby. We all listened to his story with envy.

Did some serious stretching tonight and plan on having a lot of coffee in the morning, so hopefully I'll have some pep in my step tomorrow! Now, to go grab more water and crawl into my bag. Good, hard day today. A lot of mental toughness required. Physically, I thought I couldn't make it. Nothing felt right. But one step after another, and I made it. It was that simple. Just keep walking. And it really was a lovely hike. Just painful. Thank you for all the support!

Sweet Dreams!

May 19, 2016

My plans for yesterday went off without a hitch! Broke camp around 6:30am and just started walking fast. I had thirteen hours to cover a little over thirty miles. Didn't study my AWOL (David "AWOL" Miller is a long-distance hiker who compiled a comprehensive and user-friendly guidebook for hiking the Appalachian Trail) guide carefully and was unaware of the scarcity of water along the trail for the first seven or so miles of the hike that day. I grew terribly thirsty two hours into my hike and, soon after that, passed a blue blaze (side trail marker), consulted AWOL and, not finding it listed, decided to check it out, anyways. Twenty minutes down a steep hill later, I gave up. No water for me. As I panted back up to my pack at the top, I saw Cold Taters coming down the trail. He caught me quickly! I explained that, if there was water down the blue blaze, it was too far away to bother. We discussed a stream coming up which we probably shouldn't use as a water source. But, a couple hours later, I couldn't resist. As I greedily gulped the (tainted?) creek water, I glanced over and saw Cold Taters doing the same thing on the far bank. We just shrugged and kept drinking.

I covered the eleven miles to the next shelter (with water!) by 10:45am and, even though the shelter itself was 0.3 miles off-trail and the water source ANOTHER 0.3, I did not hesitate to break here for lunch. It had already been raining for a while and I wanted hot coffee and soup. I was beginning to wonder if I would be able to make it to Trent's Grocery before 8pm, when it closed. Still took an hour and a half break. Had a nice phone conversation that really cheered me up. The hot food and drink helped, too. Put my rain gear back on, started my audiobook (Robin Hood) and busted back to the trail. And I never stopped busting it. Through almost jungle-like bits of ridgeline, rocky portions of ridgeline, misty sections of ridgeline, rainy and windy conditions always on the ridgeline. Up and down, up and down. So beautiful and wild it seemed to me. Saw a humongous woodpecker.

Before I knew it, I was five miles out from Trent's Grocery with three and half hours until 8pm. I could do this! Completely passed the next shelter (I usually stopped for a break at shelters) to stay motivated and hustled on. Climbed the last rocky and root-y hill and began, what I thought, would be the easy descent to my destination. WRONG. Mud. Everywhere. My trail runners transformed into summer skis, and my trekking poles, ski poles. I was terrified of falling and hurting myself, but despite my concern, was laughing out loud practically the whole two miles down at the absurdity of it all. Coming, indeed, to the conclusion that Virginia is for mudders, not lovers, as everyone has been led to believe.

Didn't even TRY to hitch the 0.5 mile down the road to my destination. I was wet, muddy and, being in possession of a functioning olfactory system, knew today wasn't my best day, perfume-wise. Immediately ordered a double cheeseburger upon arrival. Then, hunger briefly appeased, saw after my accommodations. As far as accommodations go, sure, I've seen nicer (MUCH nicer), but the showers were hot, the water was drinkable, harvesting power for my electronic devices was possible and laundry was free. Luxury! In fact, I found it so luxurious that I must have subconsciously decided to zero here the next day at some point before I slept. Because that's what happened. Yep, it's Thursday and, five hamburgers later, I'm still here. I woke up with the intention of hiking out. Packed everything up. But never got around to the actual hiking part. Kept company with a fellow hiker (maybe a drifter?) and the gentleman who "keeps the grounds" (weed eats) in exchange for, what I finally concluded must be discounted beer from the "grocery" (convenience store), the way he tossed 'em back. Heard an exciting and humorous rattlesnake story. Three times. But it was a good story, so I listened. Three times.

The fellow hiker loaned me his tablet for movie watching. So, I watched two. Blockbusters, both. In the laundry room, perched on the dryer, chugging water and requiring a hamburger every couple of hours. Always expecting to hike out as soon as my battery pack was charged. Alas, it still has not charged. I must have treated it too meanly by bringing out here on the trail or, the power supply in the laundry room just isn't bringing the juice. Oh well, I probably needed a zero, anyways. And there has been a beautiful horse grazing nearby, all day. So, I'm a happy camper.

Other hikers I knew began trickling in around 5-6pm, and I formally decided to stay another night. I re-pitched my tent (in a different spot, mind you. Gotta keeps it fresh!), grabbed another burger and settled down to update this ole' journal. Someone just walked up and handed me pizza. Bless them. Just reached rehydration levels a few hours ago. I need to drink more water! I'm up to six or seven liters a day!

The (almost) full moon is just cresting the ridgeline of a neighboring hill and the setting of the sun is causing an ombre effect down it's gentle, green slopes. The sky is completely clear, save a few small puffies, which means STARS! The seven or eight junk campers/ RV's parked haphazardly in the field where we sleep only add to the richness of the experience. And there IS that horse.

Not going to make any plan for tomorrow. I'm going to sleep, then wake, then see what happens next. Not a bad way to live! My body is thanking me for a break from the relentless pounding I submit it to daily. Hopefully, it rewards me tomorrow.

I wish you peace as deep as mine from Virginia!

May 20, 2016

Woke around 8 am to sunshine! My rainfly was damp, but nothing some no-heat dryer action couldn't fix. Had two bananas and two cups of coffee and began packing up. Ran into Jack again! It's always fun to see old hiking buddies! Hit the trail a little before ten, stopping by to see Dismal Falls two miles in. So cool. Wished it was warmer so I could swim! The swimming hole was perfection.

Easy, breezy flat trail all the way to Wapiti Shelter. The murder shelter. Two separate double murders were committed here. No need to fear, the murderer is dead and gone. We discussed the creepiness of it all over lunch. There were about five of us breaking here.

The next ten miles flew by. Rain was moving in, and I was embraced by wispy clouds as I ascended to Doc's Knob Shelter. I longingly passed the Woods Hole Hostel about two miles before the shelter. They offer massages. Enough said.

Two hikers were already sleeping when I arrived at the shelter at 6:30pm. Tried to be quiet, but then two young male hikers arrived, and the lovely silence was destroyed. Shattered. Two hours and six people sleeping later, and they are still going strong. I guess you can't expect everyone to be considerate. Especially if you opt to sleep at a shelter. Oh well, audiobooks do nicely in this situation!

Still hasn't really started to rain, just wind gusts and sprinkles. The Doc Knob Shelter is tucked into a cluster of Rhododendron and the misty-ness adds a magical charm. So cozy.

Well, I'm turning in now. My earliest night yet. 8:30pm. Nice. Sweet Dreams!

May 21, 2016

Still raining this morning when I began stirring from sleep. Leisurely chatted with Just Drew about literature over breakfast. The perfect start to the day. More muddy, rocky, root-y trail today. Once again, it was a good thing there were no views to be had, because I certainly would have missed them, it being necessary to stare straight down at the trail to avoid falling (which I still did, twice). It was quite lovely. Maybe one of my favorite sections so far. Moss covered boulders and rhododendron made up most of the landscape. Some difficult scrambles! Laughed with Westie when we reached Angels Rest and were greeted with a lovely view of....fog? Still chuckling, Westie announced that he was still inclined to lunch here and, putting on some classical music, proceeded to plop down. I elected to press on, Pearisburg being only three miles down the trail. More mud skiing! They should make this an Olympic sport and I could certainly win gold with a little more practice. Of course, the sun came out as soon as I descended, making me regret the wonderful views I had missed.

I had just made it to the road where I would walk the mile into town to pick up the oatmeal and coffee, I needed to make it to Newport, when Westie's wife pulled up! I was able to give her an estimate on when he should be arriving, and she offered to take me down the road for my supplies! Wow! So, an hour trip took only fifteen minutes! Westie popped out of the woods a mere five minutes after our return. Perfect timing. I rolled out my sleeping pad in the sun and had bananas, oranges, coffee and ramen for lunch, joined by Just Drew. He is from just outside of San Francisco and spoke of how lucky he feels to live someplace that is beautiful AND has all the people he loves. Great perspective.

Continued hiking, all uphill with great views of a landfill for a few miles. The breeze didn't let me forget it, wafting rancid odors my way. We, as a human race, have GOT to figure out a better way! Ran into Red Beard, sitting by the trail. His first greeting was "where are you from?". I hesitated for a second, not knowing whether the correct response was Nashville or Springer Mountain. I said both. Red Beard is from Eugene, OR and I instantly melted with jealousy. I think he gave me props when I mentioned my family had lived in Salem, OR briefly during my middle school years. We bonded over the rain induced depression everyone suffers there. Apparently, being of fair complexion, Red Beard mostly hikes at night. I voiced my interest in maybe joining him later if I felt up to it and told him to holler at me when he passed me later. I would be at the campsite just past the next shelter.

Made it to said shelter just in time to see the huge storm blowing in thanks to the amazing view from Rice Field. Seriously gorgeous. You can see West Virginia from this ridge and, I don't know why, but I just think WV is magical. The beauty is ALWAYS there and ALWAYS powerful. Even from miles away, it touched me. Made use of the privy (I always feel like I should at least try and use it if it's there and this one was even painted up all cute and sweet!) and made a mad dash the one and a half miles down the trail to my chosen campsite. I was literally tightening down my rainfly when the deluge began. So, it's tent life for me tonight. Snuck out during a lull in the precipitation to hang my bear bag and rushed back in my tent. Around 10 pm I heard Red Beard calling my name. I poked my head out and we chatted briefly before he hiked on. I was no longer thinking it sounded like such a fun idea. Lol. I'm a wimp. Another time!! I will rest up tonight and hike to just outside of Newport tomorrow, so I can pick up my maildrop Monday morning. Soooo excited!

Sweet Dreams!

May 22, 2016

My word. My most epic day yet. Down to four 170 calorie packs of oatmeal and 23 miles till my next resupply. Do. Not. Panic. With super low energy levels, I tried to make it the 22 miles to the War Spur Shelter last night. After sunshine, rain, wind and HAIL, I finally decided to throw my tent up at the Wind Rock Campsite- five miles from my destination. Had no dinner and, realizing there was not another water source for three miles, decided to conserve the twelve ounces of water I had for the morning. Felt miserable. Woke at 5am, grateful for no rain, and hurriedly hit the trail, trying to make my way in almost darkness and surrounded by thick fog. My legs felt like lead and each breath was labored. Arrived at the War Spur Shelter around 7am and ate the last of my oatmeal. All I had left was a pack of Ramen (the REAL stuff) that a man from China had gifted me with the previous day, warning me that it was super spicy. At that point, all I cared about was that it was 500 calories, and I took it gratefully. A guy named Fish and Chips, who I have run into three times so far, gave me a granola bar, which I'm sure made it possible for me to make the 3-mile, brutal climb up to Kelly Knob. Ate my blessed, spicy Ramen with 2.5 miles to go to VA 42, the road that would take me to Newport. Really nice hike, all things considered. Virginia is stunningly diverse, wild and beautiful.

Ended up walking about a mile down the road before I was able to score a hitch into Newport (eight miles from trail!). Some nice construction guys with a backhoe loader attached to their truck picked me up. They weren't familiar at all with thru hiking and I'm afraid I blew their minds a little bit when they finally understood what I was doing. One of them finally said, "Ooooo, like a 'Walk in the Woods'!". Lol, yep. Nailed it.

Retrieved my package from the post office (filled with WONDERFUL food!), got in a nice chat with my mom and headed over the small, local grocer to bulk up my food bag. Ran into Tumbleweed and Fish 'n Chips there and now I am somehow in

Blacksburg at an outfitter while Fish 'n Chips is getting new boots. I'm beginning to realize that the best times I've had so far are with new friends on spontaneous adventures. Seeing as how I'm pretty much on track, time wise, I decided to just go with the flow and see what happens. Felt special when I was awarded a 10% thru hiker discount on my new fuel canister. Reminding me what a privilege it is to be counted among this elite and special group.

After the discouraging past 24 hours I had, this is heaven. The trail (and you-know-who) really does provide. I'm still in awe that little ole' me has already hiked 675 miles. I would say alone, but we all know that is not true. I'm never alone. And I'm grateful beyond words. I'll check in again tonight!

Happy Trails!

May 23, 2016

Tucked in on top of a picnic table in Troutville Town Park tonight. All my gear is dry (!), my devices are charging, I'm totally solo and I am a seriously happy camper. Er, hobo? Let me catch you up.

Decided, with some misgivings, to shuttle with Tumbleweed (she is from Frederick, MD. The same tiny town where MY family lived when I was a wee one!) to the Four Pines Hostel from Blacksburg. This put me about 25 miles down the trail from where I had hitched into Newport. Under normal circumstances, I would NEVER do something like this. However, I will be able to slack pack this section easily next week and I desperately needed to do laundry due to an unfortunate incident involving my pants. I won't give you details, but I will say I was rather more smelly than usual! Sooo, I bit the bullet and hopped off my "purist" high horse. The Four Pines Hostel was great! It's a large three car garage converted into a teenage boy's dream room, with couches, a dart board and, apparently, all the free beer you can drink. I felt like I was at a high school party all over again. I sat quietly in the corner reading while drinking games were played with gusto all around me. I can tell I'm at the rear end of the next bubble. It's all early and mid-March starters. The young kids who are getting their kicks out here on the trail before entering the real world after college graduation. I hung my rain gear and tent on the clothesline as soon as I arrived, hoping they would be dry by morning. Seeing as it started raining shortly after I did so, I had no such luck. All soaking as I packed them up, trying to beat the 8:30am deadline to have them in the van if I wanted to slack pack. And I did. $5 for a 27-mile slack pack into Daleville? Yes, please! My pack was heavy because of my recent resupply and my moral was still low after days and days of rain.

Hit the trail at 9am and never looked back. Some spectacular weather (finally!) and we were in for a treat, view-wise, with McAfee Knob AND Tinker Cliffs both on the day's agenda. The sky was bright blue, dotted with magnificent cumulonimbus clouds all day. And, instead of the patter of raindrops you could hear the wind rustling through the leaves and birdsong. And the scent! All pine, all day. Until right before town, and then the heady scent of honeysuckle hung heavily in the air. Heaven for me! The climbs were tough despite the slack packing. It's almost as if I hike better WITH the pack! Went about the same speed, too. A steady 3mph. Didn't see anybody from my group after McAfee Knob, which was just as well, seeing as I had a few chapters left of "The Mysterious Island" (Verne) on audiobook. Tinker Cliffs was insane! The trail winds along the edge of the cliffs for a while, making for a breathtaking hike. Virginia is so lovely. The ridgelines go on and on, as far as you can see, in every direction. Dotted occasionally with a quaint farming homestead. Absolutely charming.

Rolled into Daleville around 7pm and headed to the motel to pick up my pack. Lingered for a minute, so tempted to pitch in a few bucks for another stay under a roof, but, forced myself to shoulder my (super heavy) pack and push it another mile and a half to Troutville where the town offered free laundry at the fire station and free camping in the park. Hoofed it a little over a mile into town, enjoying the small town feel that Troutville possesses. Was able to dry my rain gear and tent at the fire station. Thrilling at being able to walk freely through the huge engines and other fun "toys" while I waited on the dryer. So. Cool. Thanked the guys and headed the twenty or so feet to the park, where I set up "camp" at a picnic table. I even hung my food in the pavilion (which had power outlets. Score!), not knowing what the raccoon situation might be here...

Feel rejuvenated and ready to hit the trail early tomorrow. Need to stop at the small grocery they have here for toothpaste and batteries before heading out. So, I don't feel any pressure to get a super early start. Maybe I'll even get a hitch!

Can't wait to see what the trail has in store for me tomorrow! More snakes, perhaps? Saw four today! They love the sunshine as much as I do! Forecast is calling for HOT. That's it. Just HOT. Boy, that sounds

perfect to me after the days upon days of rain we just endured. My shoes
smell like a swamp. Bring on the beating sun!

Sweet Dreams!

May 24, 2016

Awoke at 6:30am this morning. Took advantage of the electricity and the solitude and put on some jams. Danced away as I packed up and headed over to the store to see when they opened. 9am. Not for another hour. Trudged through the wet grass (my shoes were FINALLY dry...) back to the park pavilion to wait. Happily, a kind couple doing their morning mile at the park offered to take me down the road to the Dollar General and, they INSISTED, Hardee's. The kicker is his nickname is Tink! Everyone calls him that. Except his niece, who calls him, get this, Tank. Unreal, right?! You should have seen the look on their faces when I told them my trail name was Tink Tank. The ways of the trail are beyond me! I was so grateful for their assistance and for feeding me that I did not care one iota that I was going to be behind on miles for the day. They cheerfully dropped me back at the trailhead, hugs all around and I couldn't wipe the grin off my face. The sense of joy carried on as I took a quick minute to call my mother regarding a maildrop and ended up having a very encouraging conversation. Thanks mom! I told her about my new dream: to rescue two wild mustangs, take them to her family's Montana ranch for training and attempt the PCT on horseback (since it IS a working equestrian trail and hiking it seems to be what everyone else in America wants to do). She laughed and laughed. "It's perfect!" she exclaimed. She knows me well.

The joy quickly turned into beads of sweat rolling down my face, back, arms. I wouldn't trade it for anything. LOVE the sun! More rollercoaster today. I keep expecting it to get easier and it's not. At all. Not much human interaction today. I'm getting used to only seeing most people once. That's the sad part about going fast. Did have a cool moment at the Bobblets Gap Shelter, where I stopped briefly for water. Two of the women there were from Nashville! Small world, huh?! We laughed and discussed life in Music City. They were only section hiking and wished me luck as I hit the trail again.

The last few miles to the Cove Mountain Shelter were glorious torture. There is no water source at this location, so I was forced to carry three liters 3.5 miles up and down a mountain. Not fun. I have raw hip bones now. But the glorious part was the sunset, which caused me to forget all my suffering and bask in its glow. Rippling mountains that I thought only existed in places like Vermont stretched on forever, tickled with lovely shades of pink, purple, red, orange and unbelievable.

Only three other hikers here tonight (must be the lack of a water source). Diana immediately brought to my attention how nice the privy was. I proceeded to ask her if she was a thru-hiker and, upon her response in the affirmative, I commented that I should have known by her privy comment. We both laughed at the truth in that!

Mac 'n cheese for dinner, plenty of water and I'm hoping to be in bed before ten. Not bad! Trying to crush big miles tomorrow, hoping to reach Waynesboro by Saturday night or Sunday morning.

Happy Trails!

May 25, 2016

Begrudgingly dragged myself out of my sweaty sleeping bag at 6:20am. Started morning preparations just as the sky started precipitating. Hurriedly took down my bear bag and finished packing up in the shelter. I tried not to disturb the other two hikers, but I'm pretty sure I did wake them. They were gracious enough to smile, though. More than I'm usually capable of that early in the morning. I noticed they were hiking for Wounded Warrior, which made me proud and happy.

The rain let up a little, so I was able to prepare hot breakfast and coffee, hitting the trail at 7:30am. The damp didn't hold off for long and didn't let up until about 9:30am. Apparently, I missed out on a pizza party at one shelter I passed. Never thought I would say this, but thank you boy scouts! They had brought it up the night before and had extra. Darn.

Oh, sweaty, sweaty. The first two climbs of the day were long, but well graded which allowed me to ascend quickly. I need to cut more pack weight. Considering ditching my stove and some more clothing. I'll decide for sure in Waynesboro.

Thunder Mountain was super cool! Apparently, lots of problem bear activity here, which had me keeping an eye out in hopes of my first sighting. Alas, I'll probably he to wait until Shenandoah for this pleasure. This section included passing under The Guillotine. A medium size boulder is perched somewhat precariously between two larger boulders right above the trail, making for an exciting moment when hikers are forced to scurry underneath.

Made 13.5 miles by noon, setting me up to break 30 today! Passed another trail family today, the fastest of whom are camped two miles behind me tonight. It's fun to finally meet the hikers who I've only read the shelter log entries of this far! Faces to names such as Princess Peach and Mountain Goat.

Rain started pouring down again around 2pm, just as I was beginning my ascent of Highcock Knob. And I struggled! Slow going up 700ft over a mile. Must drink more water! The rain finally let up about a mile out from Matt's Creek Shelter where I had decided to camp. Arrived at 7:45pm. Covered 30.4 miles in a little over 12 hours. I'm getting better!

Only two others here tonight. A couple from Hamburg, Germany. That's all I know, as that was the extent of our conversation. Another NOBO gifted their copy of "The Adventures of Huckleberry Finn" (Twain) to this shelter, which I was super stoked about because there is no service here and I was unable to read on my phone. Ate two dinners while perusing a few chapters of this literary masterpiece. Wish I was willing to carry the extra weight, or I would totally take it and continue reading! Alas, I must draw the line somewhere!

Stretching out as I journal, hoping for more big miles tomorrow. Can I cover the 78 miles to Waynesboro in two days? We will see. I'm hoping to really take the lid off and see if I can complete the trail in exactly 100 days. I can believe it might be possible! Wowzas! Who would've thunk?

Sweet Dreams from Virginia!

May 26, 2016

Plum tuckered out, folks. Hiked from 4:30am to 7:30pm today. So. Much. Sweat. Once again, I have miscalculated my food requirements and am worried about making it into town without having to crawl. I will get better at this! Having to ration my food made the day's two big climbs especially grueling. But, oh, once the ascents were complete, the views erased any sense of hardship from my mind. What a lucky girl I am to have set my eyes on such sights. I literally gasped and stood dumbstruck as I turned my head to peer through the trees at the top of Little Rocky Row. The valleys were still filled with the heavy white mists of the early morning, and, I must say, the mountains wore their vapor skirts well. My euphoria lasted only until I looked up and noticed BIG Rocky Row looming overhead. I'm learning to fear my AWOL elevation profile more and more. Basically, anything up is HARD. (And, unfortunately, anything down is painful!) Virginia, so far, has been only up and only down. No in-between. This might be a slight exaggeration, but that's the way it has been feeling. I churned my way up Big Rocky Row and was rewarded with a short hike through a lovely glade-like mountaintop. So green, with healthy, tall grass and delicate wildflowers abounding. The sun was really starting to shine by this point, and its rays streaming through the tree branches, combined with the cheerful twitter of the local aerial inhabitants, made me feel like Snow White herself could pop out at any moment. Quite charming.

The day went on like this. Bubbling brooks, florescent ferns, roaring rivers, lazy creeks, friendly wildflowers and mossy boulders. Unfortunately, I could not fully enjoy it because of my gnawing hunger and aching legs. I just knew all of my brand-new lean muscle was going to be gone! Eaten away by my body's need for fuel and my lack of foresight.

As I came out onto the bald summit of Cole Mountain, only 1.5 miles remaining in my hike, I saw, past the green, gently sloping meadows and distinctly winding trail, a rainbow! My first of the trip.

And it seemed to be grounded exactly where I had planned to camp. A sign, surely. I was frustrated with myself for not being able to push harder, farther and it's as if The Almighty was saying, "Peace and rest are allowed". So, I capitulated and resigned myself completely to only hiking 30 miles. And I was okay with it. A release from the pressure I felt. And if I hadn't camped here, I would not be the proud new owner of a gallon Ziplock of chicken jerky. Thank you, car campers! So, it worked out! Now, I'll see how I feel in the morning and either push for 40 and into town on Sunday morning, or I will just have to be picked up outside of town. Either way, I'm stoked for another "zero" and to walk those miles I missed a few days ago!

Sweet Dreams from (still) Virginia!

May 27, 2016

Broke camp around 6:30am. When I crawled out of my tent at 5:45am, I realized the campsite had been invaded during the night! Boy scouts everywhere. But they were in uniform, neck scarves and all, so I felt inclined to forgive them on grounds of cuteness. I longingly hiked past their elaborate breakfast set up, tossed back a couple pouches of dried oatmeal and looked ahead to what the day would bring me. The trail was gentle for the first 8 miles or so. Weaving along the sides of wooded hills, lush and verdant. The ferns, carpeting the forest floor, standing straight at attention like good soldiers as far as the eye could see. Caught glimpses of four large woodpeckers in their funny, bobbing flight. Letting gravity pull them almost two feet down in between wing flaps, which pulled them back up about two feet, as they hurtled through the trees. I could see the cartoonish appeal. Chatted with a few squirrels munching on nuts in nearby trees, almost squashed a couple toads and briefly saw a mouse before it scurried under a rotting log. Stopped briefly at the Seeley-Woodworth Shelter, more out of habit than anything else, since I didn't have snacks or need water, and chatted with a few chipper hikers I had never met. We discussed Will Ferrell and the NYC-AT train. After fifteen minutes, or so, I headed back out, looking forward to Spy Rock. Alas, Memorial Day weekend. The wide trail up to the lookout was packed with day hikers, all of which were seemingly accompanied by a toddler. It did make me feel good to breeze past them, pack and all, at what I thought was a dreadfully slow pace, when they were only toting water bottles. I guess I'm in better shape than I realized. I decided not to visit the famous rock outcropping when I arrived at the top, knowing it was bound to be packed, and headed on down the trail. I was run off the trail on five separate occasions by day hikers, while I was struggling up stone stairs and they were bouncing down them (again, water bottles their only extra weight), and I decided I should have worn a sign around my neck reading "UPHILL HIKERS HAVE RIGHT OF WAY". When

I realized I was getting angry at this, I decided it wasn't worth it and started pulling off trail as soon as I saw another group coming. These breaks, to which I was unaccustomed, were nice, and since I knew I couldn't make big miles anyways that day because of lack of calories, I enjoyed them to the fullest, smiling my most pleasant smile to each one of these bruisers.

Made the last .9 mile climb up to The Priest Shelter at an achingly slow pace, hungry and thirsty. This shelter log doubles as a trail "confessional" (it being The Priest Shelter, and all) and reading these entries was hilariously entertaining. My favorite: "Forgive me father, for I have sinned. I ate someone else's food and tore a hole in their bag in order to direct the blame to the mice." Nice. I read that one out loud and it was greeted with uproarious laughter and "genius!".

I was also given two protein bars and two tortillas with Sunbutter, for which I was not allowed to make financial restitution. "Pay it forward" was the only stipulation. I like how life works out here.

Jogged the 4 miles down the other side of the mountain behind three trail runners, pretending I was part of their team. My pack gives me momentum and I wasn't even breathing hard (although my knees WERE a little jarred). It was only 2.5 uphill miles from the bottom of this hill I had just descended to the shelter where I planned to stay, so I ate my gifted bars and headed on. Found a Jolly Rancher on the ground and squealed in delight as I unwrapped it and popped it in my mouth. Something I don't think I ever would have done before this hike. It was divine. Cherry, my favorite.

1.7 miles into this hike there is an off trail. I had planned to stop here and drink my remaining half liter of water and was doing just that when I stopped short. This off trail was also a shortcut to the shelter AFTER the one I had planned to stop at. Eight MILES after. And this trail took you there in three. I am ashamed to say how tempted I was. I even looked around and, seeing I was alone, thought "nobody would ever know...". But I didn't do it. I trudged on, following the blessed white blazes. Still debating turning around and taking the shortcut until .2 down the trail. I'm shocked at how easily I'm tempted! Here I am, a self-proclaimed purist, slack packing and considering shortcuts. So weak. BUT I didn't do it. And that felt important.

Although there are only two of us sleeping IN the shelter (Chicken Feet from Vietnam and myself), there must be at least fifty weekend campers here in the vicinity. And ten dogs. The three of us thru hikers are sorely outnumbered. What a hoot.

There is a section hiker here, though, who thru hiked in 2010 and ran into Chicken Feet (he loves chicken feet!) two months ago at Lance Creek. What a reunion! Chicken Feet didn't even recognize Rainbow Express! He (Rainbow Express) is back on the trail because his son, Skywalker, is thru hiking this year. He has lost 40 pounds, is no longer injecting insulin and has successfully rehabbed his injured knee so that it no longer requires surgical attention. Wow. He couldn't stop grinning as Chicken Feet exclaimed over and over that he looked MORE than 100% better since he saw him two months ago. The joy flows deep in my heart observing this scene. Ah, the magic of the trail strikes again.

So, inspired and content once more to simply be here on the trail, not worrying about calories or miles or how heavy my pack is, I will sleep well tonight. Looking forward to a short eight-mile hike to the first of several AT/ Blue Ridge Parkway intersections, where I will be picked up by someone dear to me from back home for some much needed R&R. I spoke with S.L.A.M. today and think might even wait for her to catch up so we can do the four-state challenge together! Everything is coming up Millhouse, indeed! (I couldn't resist that Simpson's quote. It's one of my faves. Google it, it's adorable.)

Wishing you a joy as great as mine is right now from Virginia (yes, STILL Virginia)! Sweet Dreams!

June 3, 2016

Well, I'm officially back on trail. And what a warm welcome back it was. It literally started raining two minutes before the shuttle dropped me off at Reid's Gap (this is as far as I made it before being picked up on Sunday). It ended up clearing up shortly, and I was left slowly hiking the six miles to camp in bright humidity. Mostly rocks and roots, but quite lovely. Passed several trickling springs and streams, all cold and delicious, and I know because I stopped and leisurely drank my fill at every single one. Not a bad way to live/hike.

I'm taking it easy and doing the 18 miles into Waynesboro in 2.5 days because Slam (!) is meeting me there on Saturday! I concluded that, if possible, I would rather have her company than crush big miles alone. She's fun. And I like fun. So, no brainer, I take three zeros, make up my 25 missed miles, and hike reeeaaalll slow for three days and, whammo, we're reunited and it feels so good!

I'm so pleased with my campsite choice. I must walk about ten feet from my tent for amazing views. There was a respite in some evening rain right at dusk, so I crept out to the ledge and witnessed a stunning view. Misty mountains and a cloud filled valley. You would think out would get old. It does not. Stiffly crawled out again for sunrise and was not disappointed. Went back to sleep and woke up for real around 9am.

So now I'm drinking coffee and chatting with a few hikers as they hike by. Everyone seems to be in the same boat. Wet gear and trashed shoes. What else is new? Still, a hiker's life for me, please! One gentleman was asking how it was up here last night in the storm. I assured him it had been a good show. Gusting winds and lightning. Real nice show.

Probably going to start packing up soon. Need to get going if I'm going to make it the 7 miles to the next shelter! I don't know what is more fun, hiking fast or hiking slow. I guess just hiking in general. Shenandoah here we come!

Happy trails!

June 4, 2016

Saw my first bear! He/she was straight chilling about five feet from the trail as I was descending Humpback Mountain. I gave a short holler, and it scampered about thirty yards away before stopping to observe me pass. I observed as well. Mutual observation. It was so peaceful. I thought my first reaction to seeing a bear that close in the wild would be one of fear. There was none. The encounter was casual and natural. Totally awesome.

The rest of the hike was leisurely and beautiful. These Virginian ridgeline forests really are lovely. And I think it's the blackberry brambles making it smell divine. Their small white flowers filling the air with a sweet, delicate perfume. And blackberry brambles are everywhere. Absolutely everywhere.

The shelter was chill tonight. The conversation dominated by two lady overnighters. They set their tent up in the shelter (!) and the look on every single thru-hiker's face that witnessed the spectacle was priceless. But, we were a kind bunch and nobody even said a word to the sweet ladies. They earned their right to be humored by us with their baking recipes and military service. And one of them is, like, eighty.

I forgot to mention the hour-long deluge that began when I was a mile out from the shelter. The immediately drenching kind of deluge. So, we were kind of stuck in the shelter, the three early arriving thru-hikers reading, and the two ladies chatting. Very relaxing.

Another five miles from here to Waynesboro where I'm meeting Slam today! I'll probably do some laundry and grab a shower for free at the YMCA and pitch up in the designated hiker camping area nearby. Waynesboro loves thru hikers!

One more cup of coffee and I will hit the trail. It's humid, but not hot yet. I'm looking forward to sunshine today!

Happy trails!

June 5, 2016

Short entry for now, as it is late. Reunited with Slam in Waynesboro. A kind local took us and three other hikers to her HOME to crash! And it's the most beautiful home. She is an artist by trade and has put that artistic gift to use in decorating her home. Lots of antique furniture and knick knacks, while still maintaining a simple and clean aesthetic. She gave Slam and I cute dresses to change into after our night swim in the pool despite the rain. We had all just walked in and she said, " Now wouldn't you girls just love to jump in that pool up there?", handed Slam and I towels and shooed us off. She was right. Slam and I dove straight in and ended up mostly doing handstands like little girls. We agreed it was tops. After we came downstairs in our dresses, she insisted we find a hat from her extensive collection and took our picture for her blog. It was adorable. All of it is adorable. I'm so glad Slam mentioned I would be joining them when they were first picked up and I was waiting in town.

Another zero *sigh* while Slam's gnarly pack inflicted wound rests a bit and then we are going to crush it. We will be in Jersey before you know it.

Oh, we do get to attend a Bernie Sanders fundraiser tomorrow with our hostess, so that's new and different and, hence, super exciting.

I'll check in tomorrow with more trail talk! Sweet Dreams!

June 6, 2016

Ah, it feels so good to be back on trail! I was dying with all those zeros, but it was nice to have them, too. So basically, everything is good.

After Erin (our hostess with the mostest) dropped us off at the local Waynesboro diner where all five of us (Slam, Rush, Good Talk, Breakneck and myself) proceeded to gorge ourselves, we headed to Kroger for resupply. This is a fun group. Breakneck is from Mass and has the brassy attitude to go with it. Always bursting with energy and another great story. Good Talk is very grounded and works as a massage therapist and a bartender, so he is very in tune with others and how they feel. Hence, the name Good Talk- he's a super listener, and you always walk away from a conversation with him, thinking "good talk...". Rush is a quiet, super helpful mechanical engineer. Super brain and very interested in renewable energy. He will be attending grad school to study this issue further, after his hike. And Slam is keeping us all entertained. I'm so glad to have company again. Never thought I'd say it, but it's true. I'm glad to have a group again.

We finally hitched to Rockfish Gap at around 3pm, only to discover that Slam was missing her phone. Our hitch came back up to grab her and Breakneck to see if they could track it down in town. Good Talk and I hung out with their gear, while Rush started hiking on. We had only planned on an eight-mile hike into the next shelter, so no one was worried about time.

Slam and Breakneck showed back up after about 45 minutes. Mission. Accomplished. Now, to hike.

We registered individually at the Shenandoah back country camping permit station and off we were. Good Talk immediately took off and was soon out of sight. I dropped back because I decided to stop at two separate springs to wet my whistle. I quickly caught up with Slam and Breakneck and we hiked together until we encountered a cell tower. Breakneck and Slam had their packs off before I knew it and were intent on a climb. I demurred, chuckling at how I was showing my age, and hiked on. Caught up with Good Talk at the shelter, which was full! So many section hikers! The Ridgerunner told us we could camp two miles down the trail but warned us we would need to take water for tonight and to cover ten miles in the morning, because there were no more sources until then. Cool. Adding eight pounds of water weight to my twentyish pounds of food weight sounds like a fun game! But I feel good. My legs feel strong and were steady and seriously pumping up the last climb of the day. We passed the campsite the Ridgerunner had told us about. Whoops. So, now Breakneck, Slam, Rush and I are risking an $100 fine and camping in a *campsite* we found right before dark. We passed other hikers camped even more illegally than us on the way here and are hoping we can just lay our heads here tonight and move on in the morning, no hassle. The situation is always a little funky in the park system.

Successfully hung all our food together and out of harm's way. Total team effort. Now, we are all tucked in our respective tents and looking forward to a big day tomorrow. Slam and I have discussed a thirty-two miler. I'm game!

Sweet Dreams!

June 7, 2016

Whew. Made it to the Hightop Hut (that's what they call the shelters here in the great Shenandoah). We hiked in around 9:30pm after an 8:30am start. Long day. It's just Breakneck, Slam and I now. Good Talk and Rush elected to stay at the shelter 9 miles back. Brief friendships always the price to pay for going big miles.

The hike was excellent, dominated by Mountain Laurel and Honeysuckle. Lots of gently rolling ridgeline and a smooth trail made the miles tick by. I saw two deer and one bear. I'd say that's a win. The bear was about 12 feet off trail to my left, and just sat and watched me as I hiked by. Pretty good size, too!

Hiked alone for the beginning of the day and then joined up with Slam and Breakneck for the last part. It was cheerful and filled with gorgeous views. We took in our fill, not rushing too much, and had a solid day of hiking. My legs feel so good! I was wondering if it was going to be super difficult to do 32 miles after all my inactivity, but I think it actually helped. I felt like I could have kept going. And we were flying up the last hill to the shelter. Thanks, Breakneck. It's obvious now how he got his name! He's talking about crushing some serious miles and Slam and I are going to see if we can, too. Forty miles a day for the next three days, all the way into Harper's Ferry, where Slam and I will connect with my D.C. based sister! I can't wait to see her, and neither can Slam!

I'm pretty wiped out, so this isn't much of an entry. Maybe I can find a few minutes tomorrow to bulk it up. For now, sweet dreams from Virginia. Yes, STILL Virginia! P.S. I hit 900 miles today. Absolutely insane.

June 8, 2016

Actually crawled out of my sleeping bag around 5:30am, after about 15 minutes of planks and push-ups under my warm quilt. It was SO cold. I don't think it broke 60 degrees today. So, I crawled out and immediately went for my bear bag. Still there. Yes! Started some water boiling for my oatmeal and coffee and began packing up. I made good time, I think. I had almost everything finished and one cup of coffee down before the oatmeal was ready. I have decided that I don't think I can give up a hot breakfast for the sake of more hiking/sleep time. I just can't. So, I won't, and I will enjoy it like it deserves to be enjoyed. Hiked out at 6:30am, with Slam and Breakneck crawling out of their tents a few minutes before I left. Went ahead and left without them because I was freezing. They hike fast and would catch up with me soon.

It was blustery all day. So Windy. Three major climbs and some nice ridge walks were part of today's itinerary, and it was super pleasant. Everything is graded so well here so; the ascents and descents are not so grueling. Slam and I hiked together for about 33 of today's 39 miles. We made good time, arriving at the shelter before 10pm. And we probably could have done it faster, but we were really enjoying ourselves and chatting. Some pretty great views, as you can imagine, seeing as Shenandoah is a beautiful park! The sun and clouds have played along marvelously the past two days, and the results have been breathtaking. The pictures just can't do the visual impact justice. Gorgeous reds, oranges, pinks and purples paint the morning and evening skies. With cumulonimbus clouds acting as a brilliant canvas. Instead of rhododendron, the trail is lined with walls of Mountain Laurel when it isn't open forest lined in bright green carpet. I spotted four deer today laying in said green carpet. It looked like a good idea. Saw a bear cub with Slam right by the Pinnacle Peak parking area. We immediately began making noise as we hiked and kept a sharp eye out for mama. Thankfully, we never saw her.

I'm pretty beat, but today was a good day. It's just Slam and me from our group now, unless Breakneck is going to be hiking in late. I doubt it, and think he probably just stayed at the shelter a little more than four miles back with his bros, Monarch and ThunderSnarf. They are fun guys.

Slam and I have decided to hike out at 6am tomorrow and hit the resupply store 8 miles down on trail when it opens at 9am. Slam needs a smidgen more food to make it to Friday night/Saturday morning. We will then attempt 32 more miles before calling it a day. We can do it! (I'm trying to pump myself up, apparently. Lol). I have a feeling I'm going to be extremely hungry tomorrow. Good thing I brought enough food this time! That's a good feeling.

The last few miles to the shelter tonight required headlamps. We try to avoid using them until the last minute, because they attract the bugs, which are OUT. It's officially bug season, if I hadn't mentioned that before. I apply deet three times a day and STILL get bites and find ticks crawling up my legs. They haven't gotten me yet, thank goodness. I certainly have no wish to have to go off trail due to a bug bite related illness. I sleep in my bug mask, in my tent, and they still penetrate. Crazy.

On that note, I'm off to bed! Hopefully, with sweet dreams and not thinking of insects. Two more days in Virginia. I can't believe it. It has been so stunning, and I have been so appreciative of that beauty. I can't wait to see what's next!

Sweet Dreams and happy trails!

June 9, 2016

Longest day yet. Pretty wiped. Waking back up in a few hours to finish the last 40-mile section of our 120 miles in three days. Slam and I lolly-gagged for most of the day, insuring the necessity of night hiking. Hiked out of camp at 7:15am and hiked until 1:15am. Glorious day to hike. My favorite part was right after it got dark and we were hiking through this large field. The stars were crystal clear, the moon sharp and bright and hundreds of lightning bugs were signaling all around us. Slam and I stopped, turned off our lights and just gaped. It was beyond perfect. Hopefully, tomorrow I can go into more detail about today. I will say, though, that there was a blackberry milkshake and trail magic involved. For now, I'm cowboy crashing somewhere near a shelter that we haven't seen yet, shoveling as much food as I can into my mouth and preparing to keep hiking at 5 am. I'm glad I waited for Slam, and I'm grateful for the challenge.

Sweet Dreams for one last night from Virginia!

June 10, 2016

Did it. 120 miles in 3 days. Crazy. And I feel strong. My legs are moving well, and I feel as if I could walk forever (just, please, don't let it be all uphill). The last few miles of road walk tonight were pain free. A strange sensation, seeing as I have been in pain every step of the trail since I started. And I'm sure that I will be again, but, for now, the confidence I gained from doing serious big girl miles the past few days makes it worthwhile.

Slam is in rough shape, but she has guts, so I'm not too worried about her falling behind. Breakneck and Monarch are tired but feeling strong. A zero tomorrow will set us up well for our modified "four state challenge". Instead of backtracking the 2.4 miles back to the VA/WV border and hiking through VA, WV and MD to PA in one day (44 miles), we will start here in Harper's Ferry, up the ante and go 50 miles in one day. We are crazy. But I can't tell you how fun it is. We are all competitive and enjoy physical and mental challenge, so we are having a blast pushing the limits. Hopefully, we can stick together for a while.

The hike was ridiculously difficult today. I left camp first at 7:15am, sure that a head start was necessary for me to finish with these youngbloods. I didn't see anyone else for ten hours. Breakneck finally came sprinting down the trail with about 18 miles to go to Harper's Ferry. I was so relieved to see a familiar face. Apparently, Slam and Monarch were coming up just a little slower, but the plan was still the same. So, we crushed it. Just kept walking. We still had two hills left in "The Rollercoaster"- a 13.5 mile stretch of trail with steep ascents and descents crammed right against each other. It was brutal and I had been terrified of it for all three days of the challenge. But, after hours and hours I had finally sweated my way through. The rest was basically downhill and Breakneck and I thought we could just cruise. Wrong. It was a rock minefield. So many jammed toes, "rock bites" (when a loose stone you trip over hits you sharply above your shoe on your already sore feet) and muttered curses later (accidental on my part...but I'm pretty sure Breakneck was BORN cursing like a sailor) and we finally broke out of the woods and beheld the mighty Shenandoah River. It was 1am. But, despite the darkness, the river was still a powerful sight. We stood for ten minutes with no headlamps and just looked. Breakneck said he had never seen a river that big. I told him the Mississippi would blow his mind.

Saw tons of deer today. The ones at night scared us, until we realized they weren't bears. More huge, bright green fern and honeysuckle. The trees (White Oak, I believe) right outside of Harper's Ferry were so huge! Giants!

My dad is here in town, staying in the same hotel as the four of us and has rented a car to help us resupply and take me to see our old stomping ground, Middletown, MD and head into DC for some possible sightseeing. I am so happy I get to see him! I can't wait to spend some good time together. I miss him!

Will check back in tomorrow!

Happy Trails from WEST VIRGINIA!

June 11, 2016

What a great two days. Spent all yesterday with my dad exploring D.C. He's such a pro at rapid fire sightseeing! You would have thought he was a local the way he navigated through the city, avoiding parade traffic, to hit every spot on our itinerary. I was so proud and content. My energy lasted until about 9pm and I hit the wall. After three big days of hiking on very little sleep I was exhausted. We grabbed some grub and headed back to Harper's Ferry. He offered me some last words of encouragement and support (I can't even describe the impact his words had on my heart. Almost as if a broken part of my heart I had been jealously guarding for years and years was brushed by the faintest whisper of reassurance that healing was not far off.) and headed back to Dulles for his flight home.

I postponed sleep and got my gear in order. Washed my dishes, did my laundry and made sure my food supply was on point. Kept tripping over all the gear that had exploded from all our packs and was now lying strewn haphazardly on every open surface, especially the floor, of the room the four of us were sharing because I was so tired. You would have thought I had been imbibing with the others. Promptly fell fast asleep as soon as I touched the bed.

This morning we were scrambling to make the 11am check out time. Monarch was for sure hiking out today and the rest of us were taking another zero before our 50 mile attempt. At 11:30am we gave up and decided to just re-book the room. Walked into town for a bite and to let Slam register at the Conservancy and grab a new pair of kicks at the outfitter. It turned into a wonderful, leisurely day with lots of great conversation and laughs. We met some interesting people and answered questions from curious tourists on the Conservancy's porch. At one point it struck me that we were practically holding court. How bizarre to be in situations like this when I've only ever read about them. Another reminder to wake up to the dream that is finally coming true. I'm here, I'm doing it, I'm loving it. I'm so grateful for those that have gone before and thought to preserve this opportunity for later generations. The opportunity to venture into the unknown, to find oneself, to be immersed in nature, to grow and be challenged, to expand one's community. The trail is truly to be treasured.

We plan on being in the lobby tomorrow morning at 6:30am, right when they open the doors for breakfast. Fifty miles! We need lots of eggs, bacon and waffles! Monarch hiked out this afternoon so that he could meet us at the shelter we are shooting for. I'm glad he will be there. It's always sad when you lose a member of your group!

I feel rested and strong. Trying to cram down the calories as I write this. So much water! Doing all I can to make sure I make it tomorrow. The lid is about to come off. Let's see what happens, shall we?

June 12, 2016

What an exciting two days it has been! Did NOT complete the 50-mile challenge. We ended up hiking out of Harper's Ferry at 2:30pm to begin the challenge. I love this town. So quaint and historical. I felt like Felicity from the American Girls Collection. Colonial buildings lining cobbled streets, an aura of historical significance permeating the air and a few costumed tour guides made this experience purely American in a special way.

Breakneck hiked ahead and it was Slam and I on our own. Again. I could not stop yawning. Five nights of less than four hours of sleep was not compounding in my interest. The trail continued to be strewn with rocks and I was feeling super drowsy. I decided on a power nap at the halfway point, and Slam was gracious enough to keep watch and a timer for me as I cowboyed up trail side for 30 minutes. I did NOT feel like crawling out from under my quilt when she gave the word. I felt better, though, when we started moving again, and decided to keep walking and see how far I could make it. Slam had said she felt energized, and I was hoping I could ride that energy somehow. Three miles later, however, she began commenting that her leg was dead, her eyes were rolling back in her head from exhaustion and Breakneck was texting her about a difficult to navigate boulder field ahead. We needed to abort. Our bodies were telling us that a fifty-mile challenge should be saved for another day. We stumbled into the shelter around 4:30am and, trying to be as quiet as we could, found some flattish ground to cowboy on. We agreed we would sleep until 6:30am and keep moving. Hah. I rolled over at 6am, 7am, 8am, 9am and 10am to see Slam still sleeping away. I was more than happy to continue resting as well! As the lunch crowd began trickling in, we stirred and leisurely prepared breakfast and coffee, chatting with the hikers we knew. I'm back to the front of the bubble I was passing when I decided to wait for Slam, and the confusion on the hikers' faces when they saw me again was humorous.

We finally began hiking again around 11:30am. Lovely weather and beautiful landscapes made this hike into PA feel special. I was ahead for most of the day, just cruising. Stopped at Deer Lick shelter for a bite to eat before attacking the 10 miles into Fayettesville, where my maildrop awaited. Chicken Feet was there! I was so happy to see him again. He is doing well and had changed his original plan to flip flop at Harper's Ferry and was continuing north. Way to go! I'm sure he will make it! Slam pulled up about 20 minutes after me and she finally got to meet him, the hiker who saved my life with a honey bun. It was pleasant dinner.

Took off from the shelter, determined to make the 3 trail miles and 1 road mile to the hostel where Breakneck and Monarch were waiting in 3 hours. Most of the trail was for cruising, but two big climbs and another boulder field slowed me down. I was grateful for a well blazed trail, seeing as it was dark and the boulders didn't provide any clear sense of direction. Made the hike in 3.25 hours. I was happy and felt good. Another no Advil day!

Immediately took a nice hot shower (I defeat the purpose of this when I immediately put my stinky trail cloths right back on) and came down to wait for Slam with Breakneck. She finally rolled in about an hour later. Barely even hobbling. Grimacing, she removed the gauze from the blister on top of her left foot and we all knew. This was bad. Doctor bad. She was trying to keep a brave face, but you could tell she was hurting and worried about what this would mean for her trip. She will try to see a doctor tomorrow. I fell asleep as soon as I touched the bed.

Woke at 10am, having decided that I would let my body sleep if it needed. Monarch was about to head out and I wished him happy trails. He will be taking a few zeros in Carlisle, PA to spend time with family and friends, so hopefully we will run into each other again, soon. Shuttled into town to resupply and am now updating my journal as I scarf down yet another hamburger and fries. It's raining out and I only have either 10 or 17 miles to go today, so I'm just relaxing. Slam is zeroing at least once, so this could be the end of our journey together. It was short, but sweet. I hope her dreams come true. Happy trails from Pennsylvania!

June 13, 2016

Greetings from Darlington Shelter, home of the "Taj Mahal" of privies. At least, that's what my guidebook says. It's sunny and I'm taking a minute to dry out my gear and write before I head down into Duncannon to grab a bite and a few resupply items. The trail goes right through town!

Slam ended up going to the doctor on Wednesday, so I hiked out late, making it ten miles to the Birch Run Shelter. Tented up by the creek and enjoyed a leisurely dinner while reading. Fell asleep around 10pm. Hiked out the next morning around 6am. The gentleman next to me was just stirring as I hiked out and it was none other than my spicy ramen savior. I have seen him three times since he gifted me with that soup when I was out of food and each time, I thank him and thank him and he just smiles and shakes his head. "No problem, it was extra", he says.

It began thunder storming fifteen minutes into my hike. The cracks of thunder were so loud on the ridge, and as I kept hiking up, into it, I wondered if I was crazy for doing so. But just keep walking. The rain finally let up for a little bit, right before I crossed railroad tracks that seemed to be bustling with activity. Briefly paused to rapidly apply deet before the mosquitoes that had appeared out of nowhere ate me alive. I asked the nearby railway worker what they were doing with the trains, and he explained that, because the hill was so steep, they could only take so many cars up at a time. Fifteen when dry and eight when it was wet. So interesting! He was also a civil war reenactor who had been to Franklin, TN near my hometown. Small world out here!

Hit Boiling Springs and ten or so miles of FLAT GROUND. Incredible. The trail rolling through corn and wheat fields, dark patches of forest in between said fields and crossing many country roads. It felt super American, too, just like Harper's Ferry, but in its own way. I knew I had one more big climb before the next shelter and my feet, because it had been raining all day, were beginning to get pretty raw, soggy and painful. I wanted to try and push it the six or seven miles past the shelter to make 50 for the day, but I also didn't want to damage my feet too badly, seeing as I had only reached the halfway (!) point that day. So, I took a short break under a tunnel right before the climb to let my feet dry out and get some respite from the rain. Oh yes, it was raining again. It rained three separate times. And it was 11:30pm at this point. I took off my raincoat and could see vast amounts of steam rising from my body and swirling in the beam of my headlamp. Decided to leave it off for the climb. An easy (albeit, dark) climb to the shelter. There were two folks sleeping inside, so I quietly made my way up the hill a bit to tent it. The inside of my tent was remarkably dry, all things considered. I used my long johns to wipe up any excess moisture. Good to go! Ate so much food, hung a good-looking bear bag and passed out.

Woke this morning to sunshine, and, as you know, am still here enjoying it. The birds are chattering away, and the breeze is rustling the leaves in the most delightful way. Wish I could stay, but there is still so much to see!

Happy trails from Pennsylvania!

June 18, 2016

I usually don't update from town, preferring to keep my trail journal a TRAIL journal, but town life becomes compelling and a rich part of this journey, and so, I feel compelled to share. And, technically, I'm still on trail since I'm sitting right next to the portion that runs straight through town. Town and trail collide again! This is the fourth town that the trail has passed right through (Hot Springs, Damascus, Harper's Ferry) and each town has had serious character.

I ended up hiking out yesterday around 1pm. It was hot, rocky and glorious. I caught sudden movement in the woods to my left about two miles into my hike. It was a fawn! A berserk fawn. Running in circles in the woods. Then, without warning, it was frozen on the trail, seven feet from me. I held my breath. It was trembling and panting. Gazing at me so intently, trying to place me. Friend or foe? Friend or foe? I reached for my camera and broke the spell. When I looked up, the dear thing was almost out of sight, scampering down the trail.

All sweated out, I reached town, still indecisive as to what to do next. Walked into The Doyle, a one-hundred-and-eleven-year-old building on main street and knew I had struck gold. The old, ramshackle hotel was perfect for hikers. Dirty enough to be cheap. Dirt means nothing to us now. And it's right on trail with a bar/grille downstairs and hot showers upstairs. Pat and Vickie, the owners, who are not hikers, but still love us, are great! They have been here for sixteen years of struggle-loving every minute. I asked Pat about the town, and he explained how there isn't industry here anymore, now that the sled factory and steel mill are out of commission. When I asked about any river industry (the Susquehanna river runs right by the town), he just shook his head and informed me that their river is the longest non-navigable river in the U.S. Oh, right, that would make river industry difficult. I asked him about the architecture of the buildings lining main street (which is called Market Street) and all he would give me was "old". I would describe it as a mix between Victorian and

Colonial. But I'm certainly no expert. It's charming. And, yes, old. Over one hundred years old. Almost every single building in this town needs a paint job. Most, more than that. It looks nice and lived in. Just like the people look like they've lived. Really lived hard. I couldn't help but agree to Slam and Deuces' (!) wish for me to hold up a little for them to catch up and so I stayed another full day. Sitting on a bench outside The Doyle and feeding my newfound fascination with these "trail towns". Letting myself soak up any information the locals will give me. Being more vocal and social than I ever am, and all with complete strangers. It's all so interesting. For example, today I learned:

1) How to get to the 33ft cliff jump into a delicious river 60 miles down trail

2) Just exactly what people mean by "the rocks in PA"

3) I won't have to worry about venomous snakes north of Vermont

4) How to apply for a Ridgerunner position

5) The passenger train that goes through town doesn't stop here anymore. There are also coal trains. They do not stop, either. Obviously.

6) The location of the old trail into Duncannon, and the reason it was moved to go straight back over the mountain you just hiked down (property lines-folks got tired of "homeless people" tramping through their yards)

7) Who to call for a hitch into Pine Grove

8) Symptoms of Lyme's disease

9) Game seven of the NBA finals is tomorrow

10) A plane ticket from Denmark to the U.S. could possibly only cost you $350

11) Best prank ever: Dig a tiger trap under your friends tent and wait until they go to bed. Hilarity shall ensue (Learned this one from "Tricks", another one of these old trail legends who I ate breakfast with this morning at the local diner. He pulled this on "Baltimore Jack" back in the day, another trail legend who recently passed away and is missed heartily by many). I could go on. I'm having a ball.

Slam, Breakneck and Deuces are here now. Good crew. My next maildrop won't arrive until Tuesday in a town only 40-50 miles up the trail, so I have a few more days of lollygagging left before I really need to get consistent with miles. I'll probably end up having to catch back up to Slam!

I wish you well from the sleepy town of Duncannon, PA. Back on the trail tomorrow!

June 19, 2016

Well, I'm sick. Not sure with what, but most definitely sick. It started two days ago in town, so I zero-d another day. Thought I could hike yesterday, and it turned out to be much more difficult than expected. Made it to the first shelter for a break and ended up crashing there. It's Slam, Breakneck, Monarch, Deuces and me. It helps that my crew is still around. Hiking today. A little under forty miles to my next maildrop and I just want to get there. I'll check in soon.

June 22, 2016

Monarch (who is also sick) and I pulled up at 5:30pm, unwilling/able to go another step. Breakneck and Slam were already well ahead, planning a big mile day. Deuces was still with us, but decided to keep hiking when we stopped, not yet at his daily hiking average. We camped beside a stagnant creek, sitting like zombies and exchanging the occasional bit of conversation. It was still light when we went to bed.

Monarch thinks he has Lyme's and I think I have Giardia. Let me tell you how fun it is to hike when sick. Monarch experienced the symptoms of what he thought was a 24-hour flu bug before developing serious muscle fatigue. Hills he used to destroy are now extremely difficult for him to climb, putting him out of breath and giving him a nasty headache. His eyes are sunken in and red rimmed. He is usually jovial and always part of the conversation, but now seems just like a shell of that. Like every action or effort takes a copious amount of energy that he might not have.

I also experienced the symptoms of what I thought was a 24-hour flu virus. It is now the fourth day and I still have body aches and am still feeling slightly feverish. And the runs. Serious runs. Every time I eat or drink anything. So my energy level is pretty low, too, because it's so hard to eat when you know it's going to hurt so bad. And every time I start hiking it's like knives in my tummy until I stop. Not cool.

Pine Grove is less than 23 miles away and, if we can make it there, Monarch has a buddy who is picking him up and can, hopefully, give me a lift into town. I will have to procure antibiotics and retrieve my maildrop before hitting the trail again. Monarch might have a lengthier stay ahead of him.

So now, we hike! Pine Grove or bust!

P.S. I am also out of toilet paper. The plot thickens.

June 22, 2016

I am blown away. Rescued by a trail angel. Simply beyond words.

Monarch and I reluctantly hiked out at 10am. We both felt even weaker than we had the day before and were dreading the day's 22-mile hike. It looked to be mostly flat with two medium climbs. It's those climbs that were so brutal on our struggling bodies. We made good time to the Rausch Gap Shelter and opted to take a break right on trail instead of wasting energy on the .3 mile walk to the actual shelter. It was a lovely spot. The creek ran right below us, and pine trees surrounded us and laid a nice carpet to plunk down on. And plunk we did. We sat in almost uninterrupted silence for about thirty minutes. I forced down a few spoonfuls of peanut butter and some water, hoping for a little energy. We procrastinated for sure. The first climb of the day was up next. Within five minutes I was dripping sweat. Losing moisture I really couldn't spare. But we kept going. All the way to the top. Right before we began the descent into Lickdale, I asked Monarch if he would mind stopping for a minute so that I could use the new found cell service to upload my journal entry I had written earlier that morning. Of course, he obliged. That was the best thing I could have done. You'll see why soon. We hit trail magic a few miles down the trail at the first of several road crossings before Swatara Gap. We each chugged a couple bottles of ice-cold water while chatting with our trail angel, Cue. We learned that the consistent booming we had been hearing for the past couple of days was cannon fire! There is a base nearby, Cue (also an air force pilot!) explained. We had been joking that the booming was the war drums of Mordor and that we must hurry for, by nightfall, these hills would be swarming with orcs. That is literally what it sounded like. For days. (I was so grateful to have Monarch to hike with during this time because, although we remained honest about our physical state, it didn't go beyond that. No moaning, no complaining, only cheerfulness and good humor. We were champs. It was a blessing.)

With less than a half mile to go before Swatara Gap, I happened to check my phone again. And stopped dead. I couldn't believe it. A local trail angel (hero!) had seen my recent (very recent) post and had reached out to help. I quickly explained that I needed a walk-in clinic and a cheap hotel room for the night. His only response was that he would be there in around an hour. I was stunned. Monarch and I chilled at the gap for a bit, eating all the ripened blackberries we could find. Monarch was going to hike on since his buddy was already picking him up a little further down trail. We agreed this was the best plan and I was sad to see him go, but happy that he only had a little bit further to go before his own trail magic!

Iceman (my trail angel even had a cool name) arrived right on time and before I knew it I was sitting in the doctor's office, explaining to the techs what exactly I was doing and what Giardia was. They were flabbergasted. At least it explained my smell! The doctor agreed that it sounded like Giardia and prescribed me the magical antibiotics. Iceman proceeded to chauffeur me to RiteAid to pick up my script, toilet paper, some probiotics and a huge can of powdered Ensure. Everything I needed in the world at that moment! When he dropped me off at the hotel back near trail he refused any compensation, only saying "God bless you". Just as I knew he wouldn't take anything from me for his help, I hope he knows that I know that God DID bless me through him. I give all credit for this amazing encounter to the Almighty for being with me for every step of this journey and for always knowing when to send in reinforcements. HE. IS. FAITHFUL. If I know nothing else, it is this. Just a little back story...

I ran as far away from God as I could from the ages of 15-28. I drank, did drugs, self-harmed, slept around, found myself in multiple treatment facilities and ended up homeless, unemployable and wanting to die at the age of 27. I was utterly without hope or direction. I couldn't imagine even trying to live without alcohol. And I didn't care. I didn't care at all. My family (who still saw value in me after all my running) finally got me to a place they thought might help. It was my last chance. Something in me must have realized this, because I gave it a shot. A halfhearted shot to be sure, but a shot, regardless. And I met Jesus. Enough said. EVERYTHING is different now. I live by grace and not by works (thank goodness!). Three years later and I'm hiking this trail. A secret dream of mine from when I was a brokenhearted, unsure 16-year-old. He knew my dream. He KNOWS my dreams. He. Is. Faithful. Even when we aren't. That's the glory of it all.

So, Iceman, God HAS blessed me! He blesses me constantly. And I pray extra, extra blessings on you. Thank you so much for being a willing servant. You are an inspiration.

I write this from a cozy motel room of my own, straight out a bubble bath and reveling in the availability of fresh toilet paper. I guess I'm technically not a camper tonight, but I'm still happy. I hit the trail again tomorrow. The meds should have an effect within two days, and I can't wait to catch back up to my friends. I must say, I don't think I would have skipped this part of the adventure for anything. All the pain, worry and tears this illness has brought me are already worth it. I have seen God's grace at work and have seen that my inner strength is greater than I even know yet. These blessings are greater than health on the trail, in my book. Although, I DO hope this medicine works sooner rather than later. Lol.

Sweet Dreams from beautiful, rocky Pennsylvania!

June 23, 2016

I cannot believe it is less than 1000 miles to Katahdin. Incredible. I have already experienced so much and met so many fantastic people that I feel I might burst. Excited for what's in store.

Hiked out around 11:30am from Lickdale. Tried hitching for, er, one minute before deciding to just take the 2.5-mile trail-back-to-the-trail. I just didn't have the energy to put myself out there and must be chatty if I happened to get a lift. Walking the extra miles honestly sounded like the easier option. And it was a super nice and easy walk, so I was satisfied with my choice.

I don't think I have ever sweated as much in my life as I did today. I felt like I belonged in a Gatorade commercial. You know, the old school ones where the athlete is silhouetted, and their free-flowing sweat is Gatorade colored? That was me today as I rock hopped along and my color would have been Arctic Blitz. It's the flavor the cool kids drink, ya hear? I stopped over and over during the early and only climb of the day, trying to catch my breath and let my heart stop trying to beat out of my chest. Grueling. Honestly, I stopped quite frequently today. Taking it easy. Not sure how my body would react to the antibiotics. It was a good call, I think, and for the first time in four days I did NOT have stabbing pain in my abdomen every time I moved. Oh, small mercies! I surprised myself and made it the 12 miles to the Pine Grove Road crossing by 4pm. Could I make it to town before 4:30 and catch the post office before it closed? That would be a game changer! I went all out trying to hitch the 3.5 miles into town, smiling, waving, making eye contact. And it worked! Within five minutes I was on my way to town. Thank you, Bernie! I grabbed my package and sat outside the post office to organize, consolidate and re-pack. I was so thirsty and dehydrated and was thinking I needed to find water, STAT, when a gentleman pulled up and began asking me hiker questions. I smilingly explained how maildrops worked, that anyone can receive a package anywhere as "General Delivery" and how I just sent my mother the zip code of where I needed my next drop. He was fascinated by it all. And THEN he asked if I needed water. Lol. YES! He handed me four bottles. Amazing. I don't think he was even out of the parking lot yet when a lady pulled up in her freshly washed jeep and brusquely inquired if I needed a ride to the trailhead. What?! An unsolicited ride? Wow. Again, YES! I threw my pack in and hopped in the front seat. Then she insisted on buying me ice cream. My favorite thing in the world. I could have cried (I cry a lot...). Apparently, she was a high school physics teacher and when I called her a brain, she said, "No, just persistent". Lol, so when she asked me about cooking and whether I had any formal training, I said, " No, just persistent". That finally got a smile out of her. She dropped me off at the trail, chocolate ice cream cone in hand, and I checked my watch. The whole ordeal had taken less than 40 minutes. I was in shock, chocolate ice cream dripping all over me, grinning like a fool on the side of the road. I'm still not even sure what happened, but there I was, mail drop secured, back on trail less than an hour later with an ice cream cone in my hand. Seriously, what just happened? I totally relished my sticky fingers for a while before finally wiping them clean. I felt on top of the world and only TWO more miles to go to the next shelter. I listened to Ice Cube's "Today Was a Good Day" because it was just. that. good.

Caught a beautiful view of some Pennsylvania farmland with Lancaster off in the distance right before the shelter. The farms looked so clean and orderly from up on the ridge. Red and white farm buildings scattered about green, green fields. Lovely. Cruised into the shelter and knew almost everyone there! Friends! Caught up with them and enjoyed hearing about their adventures. Forced myself to eat some soup while the guys threw Frisbee. Really pleasant evening.

Hopefully, I can make it close enough to Port Clinton tomorrow to grab my other maildrop, some fuel, deet and toothpaste. Then, the race to catch up with Breakneck and Slam begins! Can't wait to hit New Jersey next! It's on!

Sweet Dreams from the 501 Shelter. Hands down the nicest shelter I've stayed in on the whole trail. You're killing it, Pennsylvania!

105

June 24, 2016

After a cheerful morning at the 501 Shelter, I hiked out at 6:45am. It was nice to see people I knew on the trail today, even if I haven't been hiking with them the whole way. More rocks and ferns today. And Poison Ivy. It's EVERYWHERE. Yesterday at the shelter we were all talking about how out of control it is, and one hiker spoke up to say, "Wait, where was it? I didn't see any poison ivy!". He was on the receiving end of "a look" from every hiker in the building. I mean, it spills out onto the trail for miles at a time. You can't avoid it. It dictates when and where (or if) you take pit stops, if you get to use your poles while hiking and even how you hike. I call it the "PAPIG". Pennsylvania Poison Ivy Gauntlet. Yeah, maybe the heat is getting to me...

Spotted a cool chair made of rocks right off trail early on in my hike and decided it looked like a good place for a break. Longstride joined me after a few minutes. It WAS a good place for a break. My stone throne was uber comfortable. Yo-yoed for the rest of the day with Long stride, Crisco, Sprinkle Toes, Yard Sale and Mountain Goat. They are good company.

Right as I was breaking for lunch at the Eagles Nest Shelter (unfortunately, did not spot a single eagle's nest, or a single eagle, for that matter), I received a message from ICEMAN (!) inquiring as to whether I would be making it into Port Clinton that evening. I replied that yes, I was hoping to hit town between 5-6pm. He responded by sharing that he AND his wife would be there, him hiking in to meet me and his wife, on bicycle, waiting below! What a treat! This gave me motivation! I hiked a little faster than I had in a week, and it felt refreshing. Just as I realized that I still wasn't going to make it into town in time to retrieve my maildrop, I received another message from Iceman, informing me that he SOMEHOW had wrangled my package for me from the post office. That's not trail magic, it's trail sorcery! How is this happening? Incredible! That saved me!

Just as I caught Crisco and Sprinkle Toes, with about four miles left to town, it began to spit rain. We all looked up and then at each other. I began booking it. Which was difficult because of the rocks, which were now extremely slippery. When the skies opened with two miles left, I threw caution to the wind and ran. And I mean, RAN. I don't know how, but I ran all the way down the extremely steep descent into town without wiping out. It was rocky and muddy, and a creek was forming in the trail again, and the crazy thing was, I was laughing. Absolutely having the time of my life, my huge pack bouncing on my back as I focused every bit of attention on where my feet would go next. It was exhilarating. Dangerous, but exhilarating.

I didn't really know what Iceman and Barb were expecting to do with me once they found me (half drowned), but I certainly did not anticipate what happened next. They pulled up, threw me and my soaking wet gear right into their car, drove straight to Walmart so that I could grab what I needed, treated me to dinner and then, when I thought I was already going to burst with all this kindness I was receiving, offered me a place to stay in their home. Iceman should win "Trail Angel of the Year" award. Truly. I might even have a trophy made for him when I get home. Engraved and everything.

So, warm and dry, showered and laundered, I sit in a beautiful guest room in their beautiful home, surrounded by snapshots of their beautiful family. I feel like I have reached the peak of the Everest of trail magic. Nothing could top this.

Thank you, Iceman, again. And thank you, Barb. Your generosity has refreshed and refueled me and the countless other hikers you have ministered to.

I will hit the trail again tomorrow morning, bright and early. Hopeful and optimistic, instead of sick and discouraged. What a gift.

Sweet Dreams from Lancaster and a warm, fluffy bed!

P.S. I wish I would have timed my crazed, rain-soaked descent into Port Clinton. Then, my world record would have been official, at least.

June 25, 2016

Felt like royalty today. Iceman had me back to the trailhead around 8am this morning. I can't believe he drives an hour each way to do trail magic like this on a regular basis. THAT'S dedication. And have I mentioned he has sectioned hiked the entire trail sans 115 miles that he will be hiking this year in August?! Congratulations, Iceman! What an accomplishment. I hope I run into him in Maine! Anyways, I hiked out from Port Clinton with a light heart and heavy pack. I slowly hiked the 5 or so miles to Windsor Furnace (no views, but no rocks!) only to be joined by Iceman for the last 10 minutes. When we reached the furnace, he pulled an ice-cold Artic Blitz Gatorade from his pack for me! It hit the spot. Telling me he would meet me in Eckville, he headed back down to the parking lot, while I began the climb up The Pinnacle. I received somewhat of an ego boost as I flew by day hiker after day hiker, despite my heavy pack. My legs felt nice and strong. It's been a while since I could attack a hill like that, and it felt wonderful! The top of the Pinnacle was crowded with day hikers, but I snuck over to the lookout for a quick peek at the view. So lovely! As I continued hiking, I realized that I had finally entered the truly rocky part of Pennsylvania. I was on the constant lookout for rattlesnakes! Soon, however, the rocks cleared up and the last 4 miles into Eckville followed an old gravel road. Easy, breezy! I was greeted by a hiker coming the opposite direction with a COOLER strapped to his back. He offered me lemonade and ice cream, stating that he usually sits at the bottom of the trail to work his magic, but today had decided to bring the magic to us. Incredible! I got such a kick out of his fun-loving and generous act. And the raspberry lemonade was killer! I cruised the rest of the way down to Eckville to join Iceman one last time. I sat on his cooler for about 45 minutes, snacking and chatting with him and Wayward, another section hiker who joined in on the magic. He was planning on doing an "in and out" (he had parked his car in Port Clinton to hike this section, planning on re-hiking back out the next day). Iceman offered him a ride, however, so he wouldn't have to re-hike and his face lit up! Iceman strikes again! We talked and laughed and enjoyed each other's company and our shared love of the trail. It was a nice break. Reluctantly, I shouldered my pack, hugged Iceman and hit the trail. I burst into tears as soon as I was out of sight, hoping he would know what a blessing his wife and he had been to me. Overwhelmed by the kindness of strangers. Well, strangers no more. My heart is full of love for this generous couple.

I never really got another burst of energy. I dragged myself back up to the ridge and, for hours, stumbled over rocks. The only bright spot was finally seeing a rattlesnake! It was coiled under a rock, but I could tell from several old snakeskins laying around that it was probably a sizable snake. Cool!

I finally made it to Fort Franklin Road where Iceman had stashed a gallon of water and made dinner. I decided to stock up on water and camp at the next available spot. I didn't have too far to go, maybe a half mile, before I found a spot. It was 9:30pm and, getting only four hours of sleep the night before, I was exhausted. My feet were so tired from walking on rocks all day and I just wanted to sleep. I pitched my tent and hung my bear bag quickly. Took a quick break from journaling to scare off an inquisitive raccoon. He was persistent. And loud. When he first approached my tent, I thought it was a deer! Really cute, though. A fine specimen! He finally wandered off and I hopped back in my tent to wrap this up.

Hopefully, tomorrow I can make up some ground on Slam and Breakneck. I need to be doing bigger miles if I'm going to make it to Maine before my plane takes off!

Goodnight from Pennsylvania, home of the handsome raccoons!

June 29, 2016

This will be brief, as I am very tired and my journaling time was monopolized by a section hiker who educated me on the American Chestnut Tree (which, honestly, I found extremely interesting and so do not complain) and the Asian blight that killed them years ago. I am still alive. Have had several low mileage days, but today I broke 30 miles again, so I believe I might almost be back in fighting, ahem, hiking form. Jersey is beautiful! I am so thankful to be out of PA that ANYTHING would be beautiful, but it really is. Tons of lovely views and the hiking is very fine. I am still waiting for the rocks to end. Haven't seen any bears yet (everyone claims that you WILL see bears in Jersey), but I saw a massive one right before I left PA, so I'm content. Still hiking with familiar faces, but mainly solo. I like it. I'll check in soon with more a more in-depth entry.

Sweet Dreams from NEW JERSEY!

June 30, 2016

Y'all, the Giardia struggle is real. So real. Nevertheless, I press on northwards. I find myself surprised by New Jersey and its beauty. Rocky ridgeline hiking once again, yet, not too rocky and with vistas to spare. Gently sloping trail interspersed with boulder scrambles keep it interesting, and the gnats that pestered in PA have dwindled in number. Broke camp at 6:30am this morning, intent on a diner breakfast 3 miles down trail. I could taste the pancakes. Treebeard and Waterfall were right behind me. Imagine our hurt feelings when we popped out onto the road and back into civilization, only to discover that the trailside diner we had been anticipating patronizing was closed. Forever! I immediately began reconnoitering for alternatives. Score! Another diner a mile down the road. Without a second thought, we began hustling, thumbs up, in that direction. Nobody even slowed down for us, but we didn't care. A mile is nothing to hungry hikers. Thankfully, business was booming at this joint, and we had coffee and menus in our hands almost before we could sling our packs to the ground. Pancakes, a southwestern breakfast burrito and home fries for me! After spending probably too much time relaxing and getting our "town food" fix, we hit the road. This time we were in luck. A cowboy hatted gentleman pulled over for us almost immediately. I sat shotgun, while the guys hopped in the trailer alongside the mower, weed eater and gas can. Oh, the perks of being female on trail, as the tailbones of both Treebeard and Waterfall can attest. We thanked our chauffeur and got to hiking. Short ups and downs, groups of kids, rocks and shady forests were the order of the day. I hiked and chatted mainly with Olive Oil, who whistles while she hikes. A Cornell grad and NYC resident, Olive Oil was pleasant and interesting company. Right before the shelter 5 miles from the arranged stopping point, I hit a wall. I sat on a rock, not even removing my pack, and telephoned my dad. We discussed my options. Visiting the doctor again is looking like a priority, as my health is not improving. But, alas, it really boils down to the fact that I only have one option at this point. Walk to Maine. The only real option for me since the day, sixteen years ago, when I decided this was something I would do one day. So, I kept walking. And I made it to the cabin I had been eyeing in my AWOL guide all day. Was rewarded with the company of two donkeys (who appeared out of nowhere and had Olive Oil and I in stitches). The stars are out in full regalia and the cricket's gentle symphony melts the stress away. Will hike into Unionville, NY (the trail follows the NY/NJ border here for the next little bit) to grab a maildrop in the morning and will exit NJ and enter NY by evening. I will miss NJ. It has been a pleasure. Hopefully, I can stay mentally strong enough to keep my weak body moving forward. My hope is that as I //continue to// wait on the Lord, my strength will renew. I can't imagine tackling the White Mountains in this condition. I'll be patient and continue my slow northward slog. At least it's beautiful and filled with the company of excellent folk! Sweetest Dreams from lovely and forgiving New Jersey!

July 2, 2016

Every step takes an enormous amount of energy. Hills seem insurmountable. Sweat drips and my vision blurs. This can't be right. Am I just not being mentally strong enough? Should I push through? Must get to Maine.

After reaching Unionville and grabbing my maildrop, I continue to sit for four hours, drinking Gatorade and water, five liters, I think, making sure it's not just dehydration, before hiking on. I make it about a mile before I know something is wrong. The wonky vision tips me off. I call the doctor I saw last week to see if this is normal. It's not. I've followed her instructions to the tee, and she is shocked I am still not feeling well. She recommends rest and a Lyme's test. I am almost in panic mode because I can see my goal of an August 1st finish slipping away. Breathe. Just breathe. Can I hitch to the nearest urgent care? After thirty minutes of trying, with storm clouds rolling in, I do the only thing I can think of. I keep hiking. It's three miles to the next shelter and I think I can make it. And I do. The rain starts about five minutes after I sit down, safe and dry in the six-person shelter. A few huge lightning and thunder bursts and torrential downpour later make the five of us hikers huddled in the shelter glad we are not currently hiking. It clears up briefly and we chat and eat, admiring the way the sun is beaming through the dripping leaves. We manage to squeeze seven people in the already snug six person shelter that night. Very cozy. Lots of bumping going on. But we (and more importantly, our tents) are dry, so nobody really minds the close quarters.

I have lined up a shuttle to take me to a nearby urgent care center in the morning, which means I will re-hike the almost half a mile back down the hill and to the road. Even after ten hours of sleep, I have little energy for this quick walk. Bob, a trail maintainer, is right on time and we stop at an adorable little diner for some coffee and Taylor Ham on a hard roll. This northern treat is a must have!

The doctor is reassuring and by Tuesday I will know if any further action beyond rest and a chicken broth/ Gatorade diet is necessary for my recovery. I will probably have to push my flight back, but now that I have accepted this, I feel a lot less pressure.

I have decided to double zero in Vernon, NJ at an awesome Church hostel (where I was able to attend an AA meeting and pick up my three-year chip!) and feel better about listening to my body and taking it easy for a minute. Crisco and Twinkle Toes showed up and, as always, I am happy to spend time with them.

I am itching to get back to hiking, but know this break is for the best. Will keep you posted!

Sweet Dreams from Vernon!

July 3, 2016

Well, I'm sipping another ice-cold arctic blitz Gatorade, and you know what that means...Iceman is in the building! Literally. I was sitting on the floor watching the "Trail Angels" movie and he and Barb walked in. Incredible. Hugs all around. I explained that I would be hiking out tomorrow and would leave my pack at the farm at the Vernon trailhead to hike out to the shelter six miles back where I slept two nights ago, turn around and hike back to my pack and continue. Barb said no, they had me tomorrow. So, they will pick me up at 6am, take me back to the trailhead where Bob picked me up the other morning and slack pack me from there. I feel like an orphan who has been selected for love.

Little Chicken (a fellow hiker) and I decided that this hike would be impossible without Trail Angels.

The past few weeks of this hike have been tough, but I have met so many inspiring people. I ran into Deuces, Crisco and Sprinkle Toes again, all of whom I wouldn't have gotten to spend any more time with if I hadn't fallen ill. I've met Jiminy Cricket, Gung Ho, Training Wheels, Tortoise, Little Chicken, Trotter, Croc, Optimistic Dreamer and a few other hikers who were such a pleasure to be around, and whose stories are such an inspiration. The encouragement and support every one of them have offered have made me really see, for the first time maybe, that this hike really is about the journey and not the destination. Their lightheartedness and camaraderie have lifted my spirits when I was so, so down and disheartened. We are all in this together. All walking the same trail. All struggling and all experiencing the same reward. I wouldn't have it any other way. If they can do it, so can I.

So, I begin again tomorrow. Still not feeling 100% physically, but the desire and inspiration are still burning in my heart, kept alive by the spirits of those around me. What an honor to be counted as one of them. A thru-hiker. A humbling time this has been for me. I was finding my identity on trail in crushing big miles, forgetting that this is not what it's about. When that was taken from me, I didn't know how to react. I was discouraged, feeling like I had failed. But the failure would have been in giving up. And I would have missed out on seeing the true worth this hike offers. Missed out on the joy of accomplishment only after serious persistence. Missed out on the pleasure of community and simply enjoying being on trail. Now, I can breathe again. Not worried or stressed about deadlines. Not worrying about what others think of my "performance". I have nothing to offer in that department anymore. No flash, no pizzazz. No impressive displays of athleticism. I'm just a girl again, hiking a trail. Able to finally enjoy it fully. And I can't even begin to describe the relief. Maybe it will be fun again. Thank you, my waterborne illness, for reminding me that I don't have to impress anyone. Not even myself.

Can't wait to see my favorite trail angels bright and early tomorrow morning. And can't wait to see what tomorrow brings. Funny how I finally found my trail freedom the day before we celebrate the day America found hers. His timing is perfect, per usual.

Sweet Dreams from a heart lightened of a heavy load!

July 6, 2016

Well, it's hot. I honestly don't think I've ever sweated so much in my entire life. The trail is short ups and downs right now and every day I see turkey and deer. There are still rhododendron (although the blooms are white, not pink) and mountain Laurel. And, if you pay attention, lots of blackberries for snacking. Ate breakfast at the Bear Mountain Inn while I waited for the zoo that the trail passes through to open. I thought the rattlesnake I had seen in the wild was much more impressive than the one they had behind glass.

So excited to see my little brother and sister tomorrow. I need this. Almost don't want to write anymore because the past two days have been such a struggle and I'm so defeated, physically. I received my test results, and my hemoglobin levels are low, which is causing the fatigue. Need to concentrate on eating more iron rich foods. Hopefully, my mental state will improve as well, as I am super discouraged.

Just saw a bat fly by and could hear its echolocation. That was super cool.

Met my first SOBO today. Excited to meet more.

Until tomorrow!

July 8, 2016

I have never appreciated family more than I do right now. From afar they have rooted me on and encouraged me. They have travelled miles of their own to cheer me on in person, never dreaming how much this causes my heart to soar and gain new strength. They say that they are impressed by my efforts, but I am the one who is impressed. My youngest brother, finding his way in NYC for the summer. Learning life lessons with poise and strength I have never seen in him before. My sister, gracefully navigating the turbulent waters of small business ownership. Forcing the world sit up and take notice with her cleverness and creativity. No, I am the one who is impressed. And honored to still have them look up to me as their big sister. So honored. I have no words. What a gift.

Hiked small miles today, reaching the concession stand at the Clarence Fahnestock State Park lake beach area a little before 9am. Had every intention of hiking on another ten miles to the predetermined meeting spot where Rebecca and Joseph were to meet me. Alas, it was already blazing hot, I had struggled to even make it there that morning AND a storm was rolling in. Then the concession stand opened and sealed my fate. I stayed put. Spent a leisurely day hanging out with Joker and Steve, who had also decided to relax here for the day. I guess I'm not the only one affected by the heat. And it's supposed to be ninety-two degrees tomorrow!

When my siblings arrived, we all piled in the car and headed to Pawling to pick up Slam and grab a bite. Two other hikers joined us, and I was so glad that Rebecca and Joseph were able to get a peek into life on the trail. They were shocked that we had all met only that day (except Slam, of course). They realized that out here, we skip normal social niceties and accept each other as friends immediately. Only a real jerk can put us off. It's an easy camaraderie I have only experienced out here. So much laughter and good food later we Yarbroughs parted ways with the other hikers and headed to our hotel. They couldn't get over how INTERESTING everyone was. And I wondered if everyone in our normal lives was just as interesting, we just never get the chance to experience and appreciate each other like we do out here on the trail. Something to consider for when this hike is over and I'm plunged back into the real world, surrounded by people constantly.

So, for now I'm tucked in cozy and clean in a blessedly bug free room. Excited to see what the last third of this hike has in store for me. I know I will have to take it slow for a while, but that is beginning to bother me less and less. The frustration and pressure lifting, slowly, but surely, from my burdened shoulders.

The outpouring of support is overwhelming and gives me the strength to go on. This is no longer just my hike. It is a chance for all those who love me to glory in the strength of the human spirit. It is an awesome thing to behold, and I am honored to be able to share it. Thank you for everything.

Sweet Dreams from mosquito free (for tonight, anyways) Fishkill, NY!

July 9, 2016

Yesterday, the siblings dropped me off back at the trail. Bittersweet. I wished I could spend more time with them. I was planning on pushing to the Morgan Stewart Shelter, but around 5pm a storm began blowing in and I hustled down highway 52 to the Mountain Top deli to camp before the storm hit. It never did. I'm glad I stopped there, though, because Pigeon Toe and Mr. Clean were also camped there, and I enjoyed being a part of their crew for the night and into the next day. We had planned on going 15 miles into Pawling and camping there, but I ran into Lionheart, who I haven't seen since around the Smokies, and she was going 30 to the Ten Mile Shelter in Connecticut. She inspired me! I left the guys and continued, thinking if I couldn't make it the nine miles to the Ten Mile Shelter, I could stop at the Wiley Shelter six miles down trail. But I felt great! It was amazing! It was fun to hike for the first time in what seemed like ages. I blew through the nine miles, stopping briefly at the Wiley Shelter for a quick snack break. I met my second SOBO! Chainsaw was so sweet, and we exchanged tips on what to expect further down trail for each of us. I hiked on, so excited to cross into Connecticut. It was so beautiful. A misting rain and low cloud cover made the last climb of the day magical. It's exciting to see the terrain changing. Growing wilder. I arrived at the shelter and, despite the number of hikers, am the only one sleeping in the shelter. They are all scared of the mice. Pshaw. The mice don't even faze me anymore. I'd rather have a dry tent.

So excited to have completed 25 miles today. If I can keep this up, I might have a shot at completing on time. Or close to it. I am most relieved to have enjoyed myself today. The past two weeks have been miserable, and I was so discouraged by what a chore this hike had become. Today was fun. Finally. It's looking up. Maybe I have turned the corner.

Sweet Dream wishes your way from the mice and me all the way from Connecticut, USA!

July 13, 2016

I don't know how, but I've made it to Massachusetts. It's hot as blazes these days, which is sapping everyone's strength. Ran into ThunderSnarf today and he was a sight for sore eyes. Hiking alone was really getting to me. We have similar end dates, so we plan to stick together for a while. Trying to average 20 miles or so a day. I'm so relieved to have company. And Snarf is great. He really is a morale booster and tough as nails, physically and mentally.

Pushed into Mass last night and toted two liters of water up Race Mountain because I noticed that my AWOL guide mentioned exposed ridge for a large portion of the trail on the summit. And bingo! Found a flat (ish) rock slab to sleep on. The view was incredible, and I knew that, come morning, the sunrise would be epic. I deeted up, donned my rain coat (hood up) and bug net and fell asleep, happy as a clam. I was right about the sunrise. At 4:15am, I opened my eyes (didn't even have to move) and was greeted by glory. I observed for about 30 minutes and then dozed back off. Finally got my gear packed and was munching on some breakfast around 7:15am when the first hiker of the day passed me. We exchanged pleasantries and he asked me where I had camped last night. "Oh, right here." I replied. He was surprised. "Like right there on the rocks?! How did you manage your tent?" "No tent", I said. "Just cowboyed". He seemed impressed and I soon realized it was because he is afraid of heights, and it WAS kind of near the ledge. Not truly dangerous, though. The same hiker is at the same shelter as me tonight. Fun times.

Made it 19 or so miles to the Tom Leonard shelter. There is a tent platform here with an incredible view, right on the ledge of Ice Gorge. Alas, the forecast calls for showers after 11pm tonight, so no camping under the stars for me tonight.

McGoober also hiked with us today. She is this cool chick from Pennsylvania that I kept running into for a few days and we finally introduced ourselves. I'm glad we did! She is taking it slow. Starting in

February and just trying to finish before Katahdin closes in October. I find myself envying her lack of deadline and ability to really and truly enjoy her journey.

The last climb of the day killed all of us. We were stumbling into the shelter. I even face planted right into a Mountain Laurel shrub right next to the trail but popped up giggling and uninjured. I've found that's the best way to handle a fall. Just laugh it off. And it's a good thing I have learned that, seeing as I fall at LEAST two times a day. I'm sure the fact that my shoes are falling apart don't help my case. Luckily, I have VIP (wink wink) connections back in Nashville and my dear friend who works at Run Nashville is shipping me a new pair that I will be picking up in a few days. It's nice to have a "pit crew".

Speaking of pit crews, I don't think I've mentioned yet how Iceman singlehandedly got me across the NY border. He hiked with me for twenty-one miles, even carrying my water, so that I could struggle my way into a new state. I really don't think I would still be out here if it wasn't for him and his wife, Barb. I am still so honored by and grateful for their assistance.

ThunderSnarf and I will try to make it to the Upper Goose Pond Cabin tomorrow. We've heard rave reviews and are excited to experience the magic for ourselves.

My entries might be a little more spaced out from here on out, as I have downgraded to a lower capacity battery charger and service will be spottier. And, honestly, it's also exhausting. I will try my best, however!!

Sweet Dreams from Massachusetts! Just over 600 miles to go!

July 17, 2016

Well. I guess I just need to accept that God is in control of this one. Every time I have made plans recently, they are foiled. And always for the better. Planned to begin attempting bigger miles today, however, woke around 4:30am sick as a dog. McGoober, who was going to try for thirty with me was delighted. Not that I was sick, but that I promptly crawled right back in my bag for more sleep. We hiked out from Cheshire, MA eventually, around 8am, having no idea what the day would bring. I felt ill and was terrified it was Giardia again. As the day progressed, I was still extremely uncomfortable, but realized that I probably just ate something that didn't agree with me. Oh gosh, what a relief. I feel like I could handle ANYTHING but that again.

We made it to the summit of Mt. Greylock (the highest peak in Mass) and indulged in a $5 shower. It had been nine days since my last. As we brushed our hair and giggled together, we both reveled in the fact that God had answered our silent prayers. Hers, for a female hiking companion. Mine, for someone familiar with the forest and who could educate me. She knows the birds by their songs, and I delight in learning. And she knows a lot of the plants as well. We laughed as we shared how we had prayed for each other to come along, and the unlikely circumstances that brought us together.

I had been hoping to be in Vermont by today, alas, we are camped 2.5 miles from the border. I couldn't have gone another step.

We stopped in Williamstown, MA a few miles before reaching our campsite because we had heard there was a Papa Johns who gave a 50% discount to hikers. I was hesitant to get anything for budget reasons, but it turned into an amazing adventure. First, the employees were amazing! Going above and beyond to make us feel special and welcome. McGoober is a huge people person, and I was tickled by her interaction with Ed (the manager) in particular. Second, a local who had been in right before us left cash to pay for our meal! A large veggie pizza and two iced teas cost us ninety-two cents! And Ed made us a makeshift table and turned up the radio so we could eat inside the carryout only store. He even let us charge our phones! To top off this incredible fine dining experience, when they found out we were taking the crusts for our friend's dog, Dora, they gave us six more slices of pizza to go. What generosity and kindness. It was just the boost we needed to get us the last few miles up the hill and into camp. It was dark by the time we pulled in, but all we could talk about was what an accomplishment it was that we had WALKED all the way here from Georgia. We couldn't believe it. I haven't felt this excited or confident in a long time and this was on a "bad" day. We talked about how this trail will break you if you don't somehow find the good in bad situations that arise. About the mental struggle to stay positive. I must say, McGoober is a godsend indeed. I feel like I know now why God was slowing me down. And I am so thrilled it was so I could meet my new sister. Hopefully, we can hike together for a while, but even if we don't, I feel refreshed and more willing to trust in the Lord with all my heart and lean not on my own understanding. Oh, and my food bag is the heaviest it has ever been right now, and I didn't have to pay a cent. He does provide. Even when I doubt, He will.

Sweet Dreams of Vermont from Massachusetts one last time!

July 20, 2016

Well, the ecosystem has officially changed. Ponds around every corner and I'm already on the lookout for moose. Vermont is lovely. Mossy, muddy and home to the largest birch trees I've ever seen. The mountains are reappearing in the distance and I'm excited. It's cold, too. I barely broke a sweat today, which is nice since that means less water intake. The trail was nice today. Pretty even with a few short climbs and descents, but these had stone steps and weren't very "scrambly".

Mc Goober zeroed in Bennington today, so I was on my own. Ran into a few familiar faces, including ChickenFeet and Trotter! Really inspired by the generation ahead who just keep trucking on. They both look physically exhausted but keep high spirits and are so encouraging. I'm so impressed and proud of them. If they can do it, I can do it!

Staying at the Story Spring Shelter tonight after a 19-mile day. Wanted to press on, but my SteriPen batteries ran out again and the water source here is high up and seems good and McGoober wants to catch up, so I called it a day. It's only the dentist and I in the shelter, with about twenty other hikers tenting. The bugs drive most hikers to their tents this time of year, but with a combination of deet, my bug net and earbuds with an audiobook allow me to ignore the pests and sleep in peace. Lucky me, no extra time setting up and tearing down my tent. It's noisy with the puttering of the other hikers for now and I'm hoping it quiets down soon. It's so strange to be meeting all the SOBOs. They are everywhere! I always ask them about the upcoming water sources and camping spots and so far, I've picked up some valuable tidbits of information.

Wallington, VT will be my next resupply, about two days out. The terrain looks promising, with only a few climbs. I'll be in New Hampshire in no time!

Sweet Dreams from beautiful Vermont!

July 21, 2016

Today I climbed Stratton Mountain. As I reached the summit I thought about how it was on that very spot that Benton MacKaye was inspired to propose the creation of the Appalachian Trail. Looking out over endless mountain tops from the fire tower perched at the summit, I could understand how someone could be moved to want to create something so that all could enjoy the splendor of the country through which the AT passes. Green spruce forests dotted with lakes and ponds make up the mountainous terrain here. The inactive ski slopes dotted here and there got me thinking about what my next adventure could be and I was surprisingly reminded of the Smokies as I trotted down the other side of the mountain. The mossy boulders and root-y trail coming together with the spruce to form a similar picture of what it was like almost 1,000 miles south on the trail. Amazing.

Camped at the Spruce Peak Shelter after a little over 18 miles of hiking. My original plan was to hike a little further on, but I need to go into Manchester Center tomorrow morning and visit the outfitter there to pick up some Aquamira (a water treatment chemical). I am so tired of running out of battery with my SteriPen AND the batteries are pricey, so I will just try and use Aquamira from here on out. Fail-safe. Tonight, the dentist (his trail name is Argyle, but I call him Doc), who is also staying at the Spruce Peak Shelter had pity on me and let me use his filter. I hope it's not too late. My system is still acting funky, and I am HOPING it's just a diet thing. I also feel dehydrated, as I am having to be picky about water sources that I use. It's only 6:30pm and I am ready for bed. I hope McGoober catches up soon! Her company was really keeping me motivated!

Every day I experience a rollercoaster of emotions. I go from hating the trail to loving it in moments. Constantly having to pump myself up and urge myself on. What I am attempting to do by hiking this entire trail in one go does NOT feel natural and it becomes more and more of a struggle to continue. A good friend told me that now was the time to shut all emotion down and just hike. I'm trying so hard! I am amazed at the end of every day when I realize that I did it yet again. Hiked all day. Surely, I can hike for 28 more days. My good friend in Tennessee has offered to drive up to Maine and celebrate my achievement with me, and the 19th of August is when she would be able to get me. That puts me at an 18 mile a day average from here on out. So doable! I will just have to stretch every dollar to make sure I can feed myself until then. My budget is pretttty tight right about now. I am bummed that I will not be able to see Iceman in Maine as he completes the trail. A dream so many years in the making. In hindsight, maybe I shouldn't have taken so many zeros, but I know it's all for a reason. And I've learned so much.

Thunderstorms are the order of the day through Sunday, so it's going to get soggy. More mud, more fun. Hopefully, less bugs.

Goodnight from beautiful Vermont!

July 23, 2016

I have hiked a grand total of six miles the past two days. Nice. But my one-mile hike today was totally worth it. Waited at the Bromley shelter for McGoober until about 12:30pm and we headed out. We reached the summit of Bromley Mountain a few minutes later and knew we needed to stay. But no water. Goobs made a call and found out that there was water about a quarter of a mile down the mountain if we followed this gravel road. Sweet. We headed down, accompanied by Coach, a fine young lady thru hiking as well. We were greeted by a surprising sight. Our "water source" was a cooler sitting on a picnic table at the top of an adventure park of sorts. An extreme zip line and a mountainside slide which you descend on a luge like sled (with wheels!). Wow. Goobs and I stared wide-eyed. We couldn't find any transportation back up to the summit but were offered a sled ride down to the bottom and a free ride on the gondola back up. Not the direction we wanted to go but, sleds?! Yes, please! Unfortunately, it kept spitting rain and they never reopened the slide. McGoober and I waited until the last possible moment and then, realizing we couldn't wait any longer until the rain REALLY started coming down. We huffed and puffed our way back up the hill right as the storm hit. It was a doozy. Luckily, we had the ski patrol warming hut at our disposal and stayed warm and dry. Braved the chilly wind gusts to check out the sunset. Hands down the best sunset I have seen since the Grayson Highlands. The clouds were still nestled in the valleys and the sun went from yellow to gold to pink to red. Blazing through the thunderheads in the distance. Magical. Four of us sitting on a rock smack dab on the Bromley summit in silence, admiring the splendor. With Lassie right behind us in his tent with the best view of all. (He had wanted to test out his tent in the squall. It passed. Although, he did have to hold his tent poles in place during the worst of it.)

I'm glad we decided to stay here today. It was a blessing. Sweet Dreams from Vermont.

July 24, 2016

Camped on a piney knoll just hidden off trail with McGoober. We built a tidy little fire, cooked two dinners over it and proceeded to gorge ourselves. Best day ever today. Hiked off Bromley Mountain, which was still shrouded in mist, at 7:00am. By the time we reached Styles Peak five miles down trail the sun was peeking through the cloud cover and we were rewarded with a beautiful view. Rafiki and Lassie (both ex-marines) yo-yoed with us for most of the day. As Goobs and I would be packing up from a break, they would walk up we would all chat for a minute. It was nice. They were the only other NOBOs we saw today.

I fell my obligatory two times today. Both times had McGoober and me in stitches. We never really stopped laughing today, and on uphill had to tell ourselves to cut it out because we were too weak to climb. It was amazing to me to think that just last week I was so miserable to even think about laughing while hiking. What a difference a friend can make.

Vermont has become my favorite state so far. It's piney scent and lush and ever-changing ecosystems have won my heart. Today, we passed through a miniature pine forest. A grove of saplings growing out of a thick bed of moss. I felt like I was in one of those miniature snow scenes that people decorate their houses with at Christmas time sans the snow, of course. And sans the miniature houses. It feels more like the wilderness out here somehow. We were both parched by the time we reached the shelter we had planned to stay at for the night, but due to an unreliable spring and the fact that the shelter was .3 miles off trail, we decided to push on and see if we could find water closer to the trail and a place to stealth camp. Bingo! About a half mile down trail, we found a great camping spot with a small stream nearby. We pitched our tents, and I ran down to grab our water. I then gathered firewood while Goobs started the fire and began cooking our dinner. We chatted and laughed some more over our meal. It's almost nine and we are hitting the hay. We must stop in town a mile down trail in the morning, so we don't have to wake up super early, which is nice. What a good day. If things keep going like this, I will be so pleased.

Good night and thank you Vermont!

July 29, 2016

Finally made it to New Hampshire. It's been slow-going, but Goobs and I made it. The forests were amazing in Vermont. And it seemed more remote. Maybe that was because almost every time I pulled out my phone, I did not have service. It felt like the old days. Back in parts of Georgia and Virginia. But there the similarities between states ends. Vermont is lush and elegant. Filled with forests heavily laden with greenery, only to present to you, a few minutes and some elevation change later, a dried-out pine forest (always dead silent, save a few lone birds) where you walk in awe midst the towering giants. It's so gorgeous, everywhere. And it seems older, somehow. One of my favorite parts is seeing the maple taps (modernized, of course, with plastic tubing woven between trees and running down the mountain with a strange, giant-spiderweb effect).

Goobs and I did a couple of decent mile days (23,27) and then came screeching to a crawl. We did a seven miler and a thirteen or so miler and then, in a final push to be closer to Hanover, a seventeen. I'm concerned it is going to take me longer than I think to get to Katahdin. So, I'm pushing all deadlines aside and have just decided to do my best every day. That should take some of the stress away. I've been worrying way too much recently. It was draining me more than I needed it to. Honestly, I've just been so exhausted recently. With zero percent energy levels. Poor McGoober had to put up with my whining and super slow pace for three whole days. I'm surprised she didn't just tell me to "quit already!" But her feet have really been bothering her recently, so she has been hiking slow of her own accord. It just worked out that we are still together!

Sleeping just outside of Hanover in a nice church with McGoober, Treebeard, Waterfall, Olive Oil and Curry. We lucked out and have the place to ourselves. It's great. We cooked a family meal of rice, zucchini, mushrooms and broccoli, using the veggies we had just purchased at the local farmers market. We also had to get some sweet corn they had just got in from one of the local farms. It was delicious. We all posted up at the kid sized table we had at our disposal and ate and talked and laughed together. It was an amazing experience.

I'm so tired, but it's a good tired tonight. Hopefully, I'll feel stronger soon. Goodnight from New Hampshire!

Update: Slam is currently three days ahead of me.

August 5, 2016

One by one, the Mountains of New Hampshire are falling to our indefatigable marching feet. The views are stunning. It makes the long climbs worth it. Still no wildlife sightings. It's been only chipmunks and squirrels since New York, really, save one lone deer I saw at the beginning of New Hampshire.

Our packs were heavy coming out of Lincoln, NH. Five days of food heavy. We managed to summit Kinsman last night and cowboy'd right on top, since the forecast was calling for a clear night. Best decision ever. The sunset was phenomenal and the sunrise, amazing, too. But nothing was better than the stars. I haven't seen stars like that since I was in Wyoming last. Incredible.

We made it to the Franconian ridge today and are stealth camping below tree line. We would have camped on top, but there is a chance of storms tonight. Most of our camping through the Whites is going to be stealth, because almost every designated campsite/shelter requires payment. It's unfortunate and strange, seeing as all camping so far has been free (besides Smokies permit).

It gets cold up here. It's strange to think that it's August and yet it's 40 something degrees with the wind chill. Bizarre.

Wowzas! The White Mountains are beautiful! It's been a slow grind, but McGoober and I made it to the summit of Mount Moosilauke yesterday, signaling the beginning of our trek through the Whites. This section and the beginning of Maine will be the most difficult part of the trail for us. But the views should make it totally worth it.

Ended up being taken in by a kind, elderly couple on Monday morning. They fed us, let us shower, washed our clothes and gave us beds to sleep in. It was incredible. And, when we woke to rain on Tuesday morning, they urged us to stay with them for one more day, running errands, visiting their family's Maple Syrup Farm, grabbing lunch at their favorite diner and doing a little bit of baking ourselves. It was a great zero day. We certainly did not want to leave yesterday. But we had a mountain to climb!

The climb up Moosilauke wasn't too bad. Only took us a couple of hours. And the view, spectacular. We sat on top for at least an hour, soaking in the sun and the sight of the mountain range we had been looking forward to since we began our hikes in Georgia. I can't believe it's here! The Whites. Wow.

Less than 400 miles to go. So exhausted, yet so excited. I never thought I would ever walk this far.

Today we attempt Kinsman Mountain and tomorrow, the Franconian Ridge. The Presidentials with Mount Washington follow shortly after that. It's going to be a rough but rewarding few days!

Happy trails from New Hampshire!

Good night from The Whites!

August 7, 2016

It has been an excellent couple of days, if I might say so. The climbs have been long and tough, sometimes requiring the use of hands up almost vertical slabs. I feel like I'm getting my trail legs again with the way my knees protest the descents, and my lungs protest the lengths of the climbs. McGoober and I trade off pace setting, but, honestly, she ends up waiting for me a lot. Especially on the climbs. Finding campsites has been an adventure in itself. We usually just go as long as can each day and camp near a water source nearby. Or, if the weather looks good, we just lug our capacity of water to a good viewpoint.

Last night we did a work-for-stay at the Galehead Hut. We hiked in at 4pm and wandered inside to check on the situation. Colonel followed us. Usually, huts accept two hikers between the hours of 4-6pm to exchange a few hours of chore work for dinner, breakfast and the dining room floor as a place to sleep. We wanted to try it out for the experience. This Hut held 36 guests who each paid $135 to stay. It is very rustic, and we wanted to people watch. I couldn't believe it, because there were six other hikers already at the Hut when we arrived and rain was rolling in, but we got it. All three of us! We froze on the porch from 4-8:30pm while the other guests ate and played games inside, and finally we were ushered in to help ourselves to unlimited leftovers. It was incredible. We gorged ourselves. I had an evening chore (washing dishes) so I worked on that while McGoober and Colonial played cards and waited for the 9:30pm "lights out" call which signaled it was all clear to make our beds in the dining hall. We settled down quickly, but there was an older gentle.an day hiker who had gotten stuck in the storm and came in at 9pm, freezing and dehydrated. He ended up staying the night next to us and was up and down all night, being noisy. I was glad he had a place to go. It IS freezing up here when the sun isn't out and the wind is blowing. Add being wet from the rain and it's no wonder thru hikers are warned to have their winter gear with them for this portion. Brrrrr. We hiked the Franconian Ridge the other day in such weather and it was tough. The trail is mostly rock for this portion. Rock that gets slippery when it is wet. It becomes really slow going. But, for us, the clouds broke briefly, and we were able to catch some pretty gnarly views. This happened right after McGoober had asked God to romance us somehow. It was a very special moment and really turned the day into something special.

Today we managed 15 miles and are camped at the bottom of the Presidential Range, right past Crawford Notch. With less than a mile left to the road, we were considering hiking the .4 miles to Ripley Falls to camp, when a strange noise caused us both to turn. Quick as lightning, we saw a large bear barrel across the trail behind us while her cub whizzed up a tree less than 50 feet from where we were standing. McGoober and I just looked at each other, stunned. We hung around for a bit after backing off a little, but we couldn't see the mother and the cub was staying put in that tree. We decided to move on and find a campsite past the road. Well, the bear made that decision for us, I suppose. We ended up finding some flattish ground a little way up from the river near the road and quickly got settled in, seeing as how it was getting dark, fast. Tomorrow we are planning to hit the trail early to make sure we have time to clear Washington. The summit it 12 miles of climbing away. And we still must get back down. It should be an excellent day! If the weather is poor, I don't know if we can do it. I'm praying for sunny skies!

I heard from Iceman! He was planning on summiting Katahdin today. I am so thrilled for him to finally be completing the Appalachian Trail. What an achievement, so many years in the making. Congratulations, Iceman! Well done.

A damp, buggy, beary goodnight from New Hampshire. 332 miles to gooooooooooo!

August 12, 2016

We made it through the Whites! It's unbelievable to think how intimidated I was going into them, and now they are behind us. Goobs and I had a checklist of things we wanted to accomplish in the Whites, and thanks to the drought like conditions in New Hampshire, last night we checked the last item off the list: night hiking! More to come on that in a bit. First, let me catch you up...

After a day of relentless hiking, we finally summitted Washington where the wind was gusting at 65mph! This made for an excellent, challenging and exhilarating hike and zero tourists at the summit, which meant no standing in line for our summit photo. Woo-hoo! Instead of continuing to hike, we made our way to the parking lot where, drumroll please, Iceman and Barb were waiting for us! They were thrilled to meet McGoober and we were stoked to congratulate Iceman on his completion of the trail. We talked trail over dinner, and they surprised us with reservations at the nicest hostel in town. What an extravagant gift! The next morning, they drove us to resupply and then back to Mt. Washington. Hugs all around, photos snapped and then, all too soon, it was time for Goobs and I to shoulder our packs and hike on. The weather on the summit was beautiful. We could see all the way to the Atlantic. Magnificent. We also had excellent views of Maine and the remaining ranges in the Whites we would be hiking. My knees became a little weak, staring at these beastly mountains that little ole me was expected to climb. I mean, they were HUGE. I had been expecting to not be tremendously impressed with these eastern mountains, having spent so much time in the west, but I was incorrect in my theory. I was impressed. And terrified. I didn't see how I would make it. But one step at a time, right? The glorious weather made for glorious hiking. All rock hopping. Just making our way up and down massive piles of boulders that form the upper parts of these mountains. When we reached the Madison Hut, we were delighted to once again be accepted for a work-for-stay. And to top it off, ChickenFeet was staying, too! We enjoyed the amazing sunset views while we waited to be served dinner and quickly finished our chores and went to bed when we had eaten our fill. Several hikers were turned away when they hiked in around 9pm, and we felt very lucky to be inside. The next morning, we stuck around for breakfast in exchange for some light sweeping and then hit the trail.

After making it down the rest of the Presidential Range and into Pinkham Notch (and, let me tell you, this was TOUGH), we ran into Goobs' friend Alaska and his dog, Dora. We decided to stay at the Yellow Deli hostel in Lancaster, NH. Because of Dora, we couldn't stay in the hostel, but there was a rustic cabin in a large field on the river that was given to us for our use. Alaska and Dora slept in the cabin while Goobs and I pitched our tents nearby in a lovely grove of Paper Birch trees. It was perfectly delightful. Alaska even sprung for root beer floats!

The next morning, we shuttled back to Pinkham to tackle Wildcat Mountain. This was supposedly one of the tougher climbs, and every hiker we talked to was slackpacking it. I think we were dreading it more than we thought, because we didn't even hike out until 12:30pm. After several hours of extremely sweaty hiking and countless false summits later, we finally began the descent to the Carter Notch Hut. It was so beautiful. A gently sloping trail winding through moss, ferns, birch and spruce. I was expecting a dinosaur to pop out at any moment because it looked exactly like Jurassic Park. We came around a corner and discovered a mountain pond nestled right there in the notch. Breathtaking. After taking a few photos, we skipped down to the Hut for water. Somehow (we were obviously sitting in the wrong place) we got trapped with thirty-day hikers listening to one of the hutmen give his pre-dinner lecture. We kept waiting for a moment to slip away, but I was sitting directly next to the speaker and any movement would have caused thirty pairs of eyes to shift in my direction. So, we endured. Thirty minutes and no new knowledge later, we were free. Our guidebooks noted a spring .7 vertical miles up trail and we decided to not camel up at the Hut and stealth camp by the spring. Bad decision. Turns out there was no water for seven more miles. Seven miles in the Whites was practically seven more hours of hiking for Goobs and me. We knew what we had to do. We hiked. And hiked. And hiked. Goobs had taken a liter with her from the Hut, me, only half. There was no way we should camp before reaching another water source. It was 11pm before we reached it. And it turned out to be a great adventure. We counted toads (14!), caught the sunset from Carter's Dome (which offered stunning 360-degree views) and, because of the mica in the rocks reflecting in the beam of our headlamps, hiked on a glittering trail. At one point I commented on how I was really enjoying "hiking with all this sparkle". We camel 'ed up with water once we reached the campsite and hiked on (we didn't want to pay the $8 fee to camp there). We hiked another mile before we finally just camped by trail. Both of us sleeping between the rocks under our tents and on a definite slant. We were too exhausted to care. We slept well.

Woke around eight and hiked the eight miles to Gorham, getting rained on for a bit, which felt delicious after the muggy day. Shuttled back to the Yellow Deli for another night's stay. So, here we are, resupplied and ready to go for our September 1st deadline. Maine tomorrow!

August 16, 2016

Maine is glorious so far. Did 11 miles today, one of which was Mahoosuc Notch. In our guidebooks, this mile is described as either the most difficult or fun mile on the AT. And y'all, the hype is for real. One big boulder scramble. Three points where you crawl under the boulders. And I don't think I've had as much fun as I did during this stretch as I have in a long while. At one point I waited for Goobs to catch up, just so that I could tell her I was having the time of my life. "You're bleeding", she said, pointing to my knee. "I know! Isn't this great?!", I beamed back at her. She just shook her head at me. I was totally in my element. What a refresher it was. Now, if only I can keep this joy alive for the remaining 270 miles! Next stop, moose sighting! Sorry, this is brief, but I'm exhausted. More to come!

Wishing you childlike joy from Maine!

August 20, 2016

I'm really enjoying Maine. After hitching into Rangely for breakfast and to resupply, Mc Goober and I headed back to the trail to tackle Saddleback Mountain. Either the mountains are getting easier, or I'm getting stronger, because by the time we reached the top I still had plenty of energy to enjoy the gorgeous views. The top of the mountain was bald, and we could see for miles. The larger mountains we had already climbed behind us and the gentler, rolling ones stretching out ahead. It was almost as if a cloud was stuck on the summit and the wind gusts made it chilly, but in the distance the sun beamed down over the countless bodies of water and the sight warmed my heart, if not my body. We are camped at the bottom of The Horn tonight. A newly established campsite that looks as though someone went through and just bush hogged a trail. Alot of the trail has been like that so far in Maine. Fresh and messy. But it's nice to walk on spongy ground and not such a tightly compacted trail. That is, when it's dirt at all and not just a tangle of rocks and roots. We have heard two moose so far but have yet to catch a glimpse. We absolutely cannot wait for that moment. We are constantly tripping due to peering into the woods on constant lookout for these magnificent beasts. Hopefully soon....

We hear it's rather sweltering in northern Maine and so we are enjoying the cool weather while we can. 70's during the day and 50's at night. So darn comfortable. Maine is truly magical.

Sweet Dreams from mossy, messy Maine!

August 22, 2016

One more climb and we are home free. My heart faints in relief. It's been super hard for a while now. But super beautiful. Maine is magical. Just how I imagined it, really. With wild weather and stunning scenery. And, as it so happens, eating wild blueberries in Maine is tops, I must say.

Last night it rained. And I mean it RAINED. I woke at 4am to the sound of tromping around near my tent. I knew it was a person but felt confused as to why they were being so loud, so early, right next to my tent. My warm, dry tent despite the storm When I stuck my head out in the morning and saw it was Goobs, I laughed. Apparently, her tent was set up in a puddle, so she moved in the middle of the night. Her tent was also dripping on her, and it was cold. Alaska also had everything soaked. Because of this, we decided to stay at the Stratton Motel and Hostel for the night.

We all had hot showers, then cooked spaghetti in the family style kitchen and chatted with Leviticus, Bear Song and Squeak Knee. It was super relaxing.

Have a package being delivered in the morning. Will receive that and do any additional resupply that may be needed before hiking out to tackle our last mountain until Katahdin. Hitting the 2000-mile mark was a pretty great feeling. I can hardly believe the end is here. I couldn't have done it without the support of family, friends and a whole lot of complete strangers!

I'm so happy I NOBO'd and get to finish in Maine. It's just so over the top beautiful. Can't wait for a moose and Katahdin!

August 29, 2016

About to head out from Monson to tackle the 100 miles wilderness. I cannot believe it. Absolutely cannot believe it. This trip has taught me so much.

McGoober and I are loaded up with five days of food and excited to get to Katahdin. Hopefully, we will see a moose. Still haven't checked that one off the list.

Hopefully, I'll have enough service to upload some more updates through the wilderness!

September 2, 2016

44 miles to go. Amazing. We caught a glimpse of Katahdin yesterday from White Cap Mountain. It's huge. And it looked so close. I wanted to just keep walking until we got there, but Goobs put her foot down. And she's right. We should enjoy these precious few days we have left. We have a family now. It's Goobs, Alaska, Colin (a chef from Liverpool!) and me. And Dora, of course, Alaska's well behaved Mastiff mix. We have been hiking on and off together for a couple of weeks now and are delighted at the chance to summit together. No moose sightings yet. But we did have an amazing trail magic lunch flown into us via sea plane today. That was almost as cool. The terrain has been so much easier the past few days. Shorter climbs and long flat stretches. Still climbing our way over roots and rocks, but that seems to almost be child's play for us at this point. One of our friends did snap her ankle in three places the other day in the wilderness. It took 24 people to carry her out. I find myself taking my time on wet rocks now. It rained our first two nights in the wilderness. No sweat. Soaking gear also seems like child's play. The only thing we really concern ourselves with are water sources, food supply and how our legs feel. Ah, the simple life. Morale is excellent, as you can imagine. Out here on the trail, the amazingness of completing a thru hike is somewhat diminished by the fact that I am constantly surrounded by other thru hikers. I have to remind myself that this isn't something that people get to do every day. So many things must go right in order to hike 2200 miles in one go. Thank you, Lord, for seeing to my needs. Sweet Dreams from wild, wonderful Maine!

September 5, 2016

It's finished. We summitted. And it was gorgeous. A gorgeous day, a gorgeous view, gorgeous feelings. More to come later.

September 8, 2016

Just boarded the flight that is the last leg of my journey home. I remember thinking about what this moment would feel like as I stumbled over rocks in Pennsylvania, sweated my brains out in New Jersey and New York, laid eyes on the North's Boreal forests for the first time and as I walked with wonder through Maine. What a journey. I still haven't shed a tear, however, and that is unexpected. I suppose I just cried myself out on trail.

New, grander goals filling the space in my mind that had heretofore been consumed by this hike. I feel a quiet satisfaction and peace, but no outrageous, wild rush of joy. It's very strange. We made it to the Abol Bridge which marks the end of the 100-mile wilderness on the morning of our sixth day in the wilderness. We planned perfectly and Goobs, Colin and I executed this section of the hike with perfection. I fear Colin was a little hard put at moments, but we kept excellent morale and really enjoyed each other's company. We decided to camp at The Birches, the site reserved for "long distance hikers" at the base of Katahdin, on Sunday night, ensuring our summit day would go off without any hitches, time wise. We rose at our normal 6am and reached the trailhead at 7:30am. We hustled up in three hours, spent about 30 minutes basking in the glory of that rough, wooden sign that marked the end of our sojourn and then leisurely made our way back down the mountain. The day was perfect. Colin, McGoober, Bearsong, Squeak-Knee and myself were all able to celebrate together on the summit. And by celebrate, I mean gaze around with wonder, silly smiles plastered on our faces, exchanging a multitude of high fives and hugs- the most physical contact I've had in months. It was surreal. We shuttled to the AT Lodge in Millinocket where we ate, showered, did laundry and tried to work out the next stages of travel. We shuttled to Medway the next morning, where we caught a bus to Bangor. And here we parted ways, Goobs to Burlington, VT to prepare for the Long Trail and Colin to Toronto to visit cousins. Bearsong, Squeak Knee and I were catching a ride to Portland later in the day from one of my family friends and trail angels, Uncle Ray, and had some serious time to kill. So, we went bowling. It was a blast. It was only us and the owner in the building which helped with our transition back into public places as normal citizens. I want to be in the woods again. What a gift to have been able to spend an entire summer in the great outdoors. I will surely never be the same. Thanks again for all the support I have received from friends, family and angels. It's going to take a while to wrap my head around such radical generosity.

Don't miss out!

Visit the website below and you can sign up to receive emails whenever Leslie Fletcher publishes a new book. There's no charge and no obligation.

https://books2read.com/r/B-A-VMBW-PGYFC

BOOKS2READ

Connecting independent readers to independent writers.

About the Author

Leslie stays both cozy and active in Chattanooga, TN with her husband, step-sons and pup. To this day nothing delights her more than splitting time between the trail and the kitchen.

Read more at shoplushlie.com.